Roger Mason was born at Skipton, Yorkshire, in 1940. He was educated at Giggleswick School and Queen's College, Oxford where he read law. After qualifying as a barrister his interest in architecture and local history led him to become a town planner. He now lives in a village in Oxfordshire and teaches town planning at Oxford Polytechnic.

D1589668

Roger Mason

Granny's Village

Futura Publications Limited
A Futura Book

A Futura Book

First published in Great Britain by
Peter Davies Limited in 1977

First Futura Publications edition 1978

Copyright © 1977 Roger Mason

This book is sold subject to the condition
that it shall not, by way of trade or
otherwise, be lent, re-sold, hired out or
otherwise circulated without the publisher's
prior consent in any form of binding or
cover other than that in which it is
published and without a similar condition
including this condition being imposed on the
subsequent purchaser

ISBN 0 7088 1455 7

Printed in Great Britain by
Hazell Watson & Viney Ltd
Aylesbury, Bucks

Futura Publications Limited
110 Warner Road
Camberwell, London SE5

Contents

TO
Granny
AND
Thornton-in-Craven

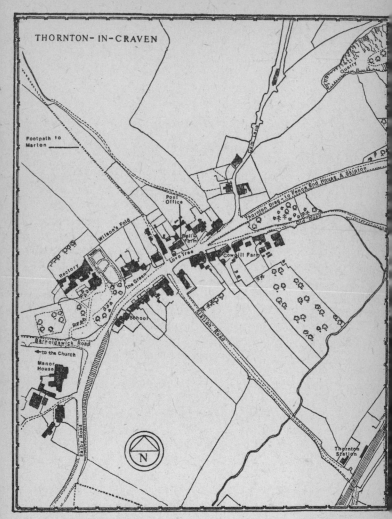

Thornton-in-Craven as it was at the turn of the century.

Introduction

The village of Thornton-in-Craven, set in the Yorkshire hills, is outwardly very much the same as it was in 1882 when my Granny was born in a stone cottage by the Post Office. Nothing particularly distinguishes it, no great house, noble family, or famous inhabitant. But the way of life, the people, their trades, and the old village families, have all changed beyond recognition. To my own children sitting with us at the kitchen fire it is a lost world, a part of history.

Granny was telling us a story, and, as she chuckled, leaning her head against the hard chair back, she suddenly drew in her breath sharply. 'What's the matter, Granny,' I said. 'Nay,' she replied, 'I were trying to read in bed last night, and I burnt myself.' We looked at her in amazement. 'I had t'candle on me chest,' she went on, 'and I must have fallen asleep. Anyroad, I woke up with a pool of candle fat round me neck.'

'Granny, you'll set yourself on fire,' we groaned. 'Have you seen the doctor?' She shook her head. 'I don't need t'doctor. It'll mend.' Granny is stubbornly independent, but we insisted. 'What did you do?' 'Oh,' she gave us a sharp little grin, 'I lay there and sang meself hymns.'

I was reminded by this of staying with her over thirty years ago, and how she used to sing songs to comfort me as I was put to bed. It was even then for me an exploration into the past to sleep in the small boarded-off bedroom, with its

1

high brass bed and soft lumpy feather mattress. I was told that my father and uncle had slept together as children in that room in the same bed, which puzzled my mind with quite impossible ideas. How could those two large and competent men ever have been so small as myself and have looked around in the half-light at this new old world? A cupboard was sunk in the wall above the bed, full of treasures, musty books, old parchesi pieces and painted tin boxes. Next door old Reuben, Granny's brother, snored through the partition wall as he had done for fifty years or more, lying there under his quilt, chamber pot under the bed, and striped shirt and baggy trousers, with braces still attached, dropped on the chair.

I would set out from the security of Granny's fireside on my first explorations of her village, Thornton-in-Craven. In summer I ran through the dust of the yard and up the grassy path to the garden to strip untidy gooseberry bushes of their ripe, yellow fruit and spit out the fuzzy tails after each mouthful. I went along Cam Lane and through the fields to look down into the depths of the quarry, daringly hanging on to the rickety fence and imagining my body sliding down that long smooth rock face into the water which rumour said was far too deep to be sounded – at least by any boy with the longest stick he could find.

Other relics of the lost past also survived to stir a child's imagination. At the end of the yard stood a dusty, locked workshop, closed by great double doors. If Granny found the key and the doors creaked open, it would be much as her father left it, with a long bench marked by his tools, vices fixed in place, and old, rusty spokeshaves, with worm-eaten handles, hanging on the walls. My Grandad, who was a railwayman, had hardly used the workshop.

When I grew older I could cross the black, traffic-laden road, where Granny had once played with her top in the gravel, and follow Station Hill down to the remains of a railway running in the valley, an enormous earthwork, broken here and there by destroyed bridges, used for a hundred years and then forgotten. The station itself has vanished, and the sawmill further down that same road is now a barn.

Piece by piece I was able to fit together the pattern of Granny's life. She was born into a working family. Her father had the by-name 'Bushman', for he was the village wheelwright. Her mother, Sarah, first came to Thornton as a cook and later made up servants' clothes in the front parlour. Granny, who was their eldest daughter, Nelly Riley, lived all her life in the village and she observed and remembered. Now, at ninety-four, she is still alert and active, interested in everything that goes on. She lives alone and looks after herself, even though her eyesight has almost gone; when pouring tea she puts a finger just inside the rim of the cup, to feel when the hot liquid has risen to the right level. Granny has passed on her accumulated memories to me. I have used them as the raw material for this book. It is the story of her village in the days when she was a girl.

1

Tales in Winter

Gusts of wind beat against the hard grey stone of the row of cottages. For over a thousand years the village had grown into the shelter of its green hillside as its folk adjusted themselves and their houses to driving rain, storm and snow.

Dark trunks and leafless branches of the trees stood out against the pale cold sunlight of December. In his stone workshop behind the cottages Nelly's Dad, Bushman Riley, blew on his hands as they slipped loosely round the cold wooden shaft of his adze.

There was no warmth in the workshop, no fire, and an open door to let in winter weather; the best Bushman could do was to rough out the timber for his spring-time jobs; for fine work he needed warm hands. Few jobs came in just before Christmas in any case. He put down the tool and walked across the yard to the back door to warm his hands at the fire before going up the garden. 'Is there owt needed from t'garden, Sarah?' he said. Nelly's Mam put down her thimble and prodded the cat until it moved reluctantly off her work table. 'I don't think so. But t'privy could do with emptying.' Bushman grunted unhappily, stood before the fire a moment longer, then crossed to the door and raised the latch.

When he came out again he collected his spade from the workshop wall and disappeared into the icy-cold stone boxes where the privies stood. He lifted up a wooden flap and shovelled out the mixture of earth, ash, and soil into a bucket. Then, carrying the bucket carefully, his spade over his shoulder, he went up the steep narrow path at the back of the yard to his garden on the hill above the village. He emptied the bucketful on to the muck-heap in the corner by the gate. Deep spade marks showed where he had cut his way into the old pile to spread it on the newly dug ground. Man and muck together had produced a black crumbly loam, and it was good land, sweet from the limestone below. There stood the rows of brussels sprouts, green and knobbly on their battered stalks, ugly but useful. There were cabbages with thin slug-marks on their outside leaves, a deep purple green in the fading light, and beyond them the feathery tops of a few late carrots. He had time for half-an-hour's digging before dark.

Bushman pushed in his spade at the edge of the trodden vegetable patch and bent his back and legs in the old untiring movement. The slabs of earth broke away easily as he worked his way down the slope of the land. When he straightened up, the roofs of cottages and workshop stood black below him against the setting sun, and the distant moors were velvet-brown, stained with long water-marks in their old coat of heather and bracken.

In a quiet spell, as the wind died away, he could hear his neighbour's cows as they rustled through the yellowed grass of the fold behind Bell's farm. 'Just like Billy-a-Doad to leave 'em out till his boys get back,' Bushman muttered to himself. He grinned in anticipation, bent to pick up a stone, then flicked it at the nearest cow, which backed away, mooing softly in protest. Then he raised his head to the sound of clogs coming up the path.

Nelly, just back from school herself, in white pinafore, grey dress under, scrambled light-footed round the corner of the gate. She halted, upright on the grass, her sharp face white against the gathering darkness of the valley behind her, and automatically smoothed her long hair back before

6

she spoke. 'Dad, Billy-a-Doad's at the door. He's a pig to kill, and Mam says we'll be wanting blood for puddings.' Then, with her love of small, safe adventures and the need to know everything that happened in her village, she pleaded, 'Dad, can I come too?'

Bushman nodded, said 'Aye', carefully cleaned his spade against the wall, and set off down the path with Nelly. He put his soil-bucket back in the workshop and took down the hens' corn-bucket from its hook on the wall. Nelly ran inside for the tin milk kit and father and daughter went round the corner of the yard and down towards the road. They could hear the squealing before they reached the Post Office. Half the village must know Billy-a-Doad was killing a pig.

At the back of Bell's farm a light shone out under the stone lintel of the shippon door. Dad ducked inside, Nelly followed hesitantly. The pig hung there on a great iron hook, enormous, flabby and pinkish-white with coarse hair on its sides and back. From the slit in its throat steaming blood still ran into the bucket below and a full bucket stood against the wall beside. The pig's mouth was slightly open and Nelly could see its soft tongue, wet with spit and blood. Small dark streams ran down the cheeks and splashed into the sticky pool in the bucket below.

Round and cheerful, a cherub of forty, his floppy shirt hanging outside baggy trousers as he came to meet them, Billy-a-Doad grinned at Bushman and winked at Nelly. He looked at the blood and their containers: 'Tha must keep stirring it, Bushman, or it'll curdle, tha knows.' 'Aye,' said Bushman. Billy took up the bucket and poured a full measure into Bushman's, and then he lifted the lid of the milk kit and filled that too. He nodded at the pig beside his head. 'You'll be wanting some ribs, I suppose?' 'Aye,' said Bushman again. He and Billy grinned again at each other, their teeth shining white in the lamplight. Billy-a-Doad's forearms were streaked with blood, splashes darkened his shirt, and when he turned his head to look at Nelly the lambent shadows hid his eyes. She shivered, half from the damp, half in fear at this strange ritual figure peering at her from the darkness. 'Come on, sweetheart,' he said, 'there's a bit of spice for thee in t'kitchen.' And his smiling eyes appeared to reassure her when he moved. Nelly turned and scampered down to the farmhouse, happy to be safe with Mrs Wilkinson, Billy's busy wife.

Billy-a-Doad and Bushman came in shortly to wash their hands and found Nelly sitting contentedly by the fire, chewing the 'spice', a chunk of dark treacle toffee. Then their arms stretching under the bucket load of blood, she and her Dad set off home. The sky had darkened and thick clouds signalled rain. Nelly kept close beside Bushman as they followed the gravel road up the village, past the front of their own cottage row, under the dripping bare branches of the 'love tree', the big lime beside the road, and at last round the corner and into the safety of their own back yard as they brought their new riches to the kitchen door.

Nelly's Mam, always at work, stood in her apron beside the scrubbed table-top; the oil lamp was on the window-sill and a sack of oatmeal bulged against the table leg. 'What kept thee?' said Mam sharply, but Nelly ran across, put her arms round the floury apron, and said, 'Mam, I were frightened of that pig.' 'Dids't tha take the lass inside?' The remark was thrown at Bushman, who parried it in his usual way, with a grin and silence. He put the full bucket solemnly down on the floor and asked 'Where's the lads and Annie?' 'Oh,' said Mam, 'I sent 'em into t'front room. They were getting under foot.' Then she took Nelly's face and turned it towards the lamp. 'Now lass,' she said with sharp reassurance, 'th'art ten years old. Don't mind blood. It can't hurt thee.' 'It's best not to let it stand,' she added, nodding at the milk-kit and bucket beside her. So they set to work, mixing up the mess of blood, fat and oatmeal until they had a pile of puddings ready for cooking. Bushman cleared space by putting the finished, cloth-wrapped puddings into the cast-iron boiler beside the fire. They could safely be left to cook on their own and be lifted out, cold, next morning. When the job was done, and the table scrubbed clean again, they had their tea. Mam always swore they spent all year preparing for winter.

In those December evenings, when the light was too bad for making dresses, she could sit for a little beside the fire with her family about her, and in her mind run comfortingly over the stores they had put away. Gleaming rows of jars and pots stood on the stone slabs in the pantry, full of jams and preserves and chutneys in black and brown, deep red or fresh pale green. And in the summer they had filled the bottles, which stood on flags below the stone shelves, with rhubarb wine, the red sticks squeezed through worn wooden rollers as Bushman turned the mangle. They had boiled it in a jelly pan, and the sugared juice was put away in bottles to ferment ready for Christmas. In a corner stood a pile of cloth-wrapped puddings, plum or black, sweet or savoury, waiting to be steamed and brought to life with flaming brandy or sliced and fried in their own juice, and beside them the big brown pot jars of mincemeat.

Mam's system of reserves stretched out beyond the house itself. She had counted the rows of vegetables keeping cool and fresh for her family up in the garden. She had watched the level rising inside the great tarred barrel at the back of the workshop, where summer's surplus eggs were stored in layer after layer, under a covering of water-glass. They might taste a little dull by the time the spring came but they kept until Bushman had fresh eggs to put under the broody hen in its pen in the yard. Then they would have cock chicken pie for dinner.

As they all sat round the fire in the kitchen Nelly and the other children would ask for stories, Mam's eyes would begin to close, gently dropping down and then opening like the cat's as Bushman went on. Shadows from the flames

9

brought out the dark rings round her eyes, the wrinkles created by days of dress-making in poor winter light. She looked older than Bushman, but then she worried about them all, about money, and about the future. Sometimes her legs ached and she would have to lie down on the settee till she could stand again. On those days Mam worked later into the evening to finish off her day's stint of black Sunday dresses for folk in Earby or servants up at the rectory. The firelight cast deeper shadows into the creases on either side of her nose and down-turned mouth. It glowed gently on her white face and strong chin above the solid black of her dress, bringing out odd flecks of light in the heavy material and in the black lace at her neck. Light shone on the smooth steel of the wreckon over the fire, pulled to one side now to keep the kettle from the coal. The black lead on grate and boiler stood out in contrast to glowing red. Above their heads was a rack-full of drying clothes.

The big black cat, its eyes closed, purred furiously, filling the room with its own sound of comfort. Bushman would sit above them in the stuffed and buttoned rocking chair, creaking gently to and fro and solemnly tell the tale. The children, Nelly and Annie, Jack, Reuben and little Alan sat near the hearth, feeling tufts of old cloth in the tatted rug, waiting for the next words in the dim light of the lamp with its wick well down.

Mam herself told them how Nelly was born in May 1882, as she lay in the upstairs front bedroom, close against the love tree. Brass bedsteads and the humming of bees welcomed her baby into the world. Brothers and a sister were born in that same small bedroom. 'I thought our Nelly were never going to live,' Mam said, 'she wheezed like an old horse.' All the women who were helping out at the birth gave urgent and conflicting advice. Bushman's mother and his sister Lizzie took control. They sent Billy-a-Doad's wife, little and sharpnosed, scurrying up the village to bring the rector. Bushman's father, Wright-Jack, waiting down below, heard sounds of confusion through the plaster. He took station at the foot of the stairs and shouted his advice: 'Make it cough; give it some gin.'

When he heard the rector's horse trot up to the front door and the rector's boots on the gravel as he led it to the rail beside the Post Office, Wright-Jack went out to bring him in. The rector still wore hunting breeches under his cassock, his surplice slung over his shoulder. Even when bustling to the stairs he moved with conscious dignity. Red-faced, kindly, occasionally pompous or abrupt, with the bedside manner and competence with children of a jovial family doctor, Mr Morris was ideally suited for this crisis.

He came into the stuffy bedroom, with its one open window pane and the fire adding its own heat to the May sunshine. Nelly's gasping little body lay in her Grand-mother's arms. 'Well, well; well, well,' said Mr Morris as he emerged from the low doorway head down, and straightened by the bedside to survey the scene. He laid a firm hand on Sarah's sticky forehead and said, 'She looks a fine daughter indeed, Mrs Riley.' Then taking the baby in his arms he peered at her, muttering: 'Well, well; well, well,' as he did to all the village children, before reaching into his pocket to give them a toffee. This was his 'rectory potion', but it was out of the question on this occasion and he was momentarily at a loss.

'Yes, Mrs Riley, she's a fine girl, indeed, but I'll christen her just to be sure.' Putting down the baby he took the surplice off his shoulder and shrugged it over his head until his red face appeared above a new white body. Then, regardless of breeches and boots beneath, he calmly per-formed the ceremony. 'Nelly went on wheezing all the time,' Mam told them drily. Whereupon, giving early proof of her contrary nature, the mixture of apparent vulnerability and inner strength, Nelly Riley began to breathe, sleep and eat with due regularity, and so had the honour to be christened a second time, in Thornton church. Whether her long life is to be attributed to the early gin or the double treatment with holy water no one can tell, but her Grandmother swore at the time: 'That lass'll live to be a hundred.'

When she had finished the story Nelly's Mam reached down to touch her daughter's cheek, as if to atone for making her the butt of the tale, and almost to reassure herself that the child was still there. Nelly leant her head back and smiled upwards in acknowledgment, with a child's instinctive sympathy. 'Tell us about Hugh, Mam,' she pleaded. 'Nay, it'll upset your Dad. It took me six months to get him cheerful after the lad died. And you're as soft as your Dad.' Nelly had tears in her eyes already at the thought. She looked round at her surviving brothers and sisters.

Jack, her half-brother, and Mam's eldest, already a working man of thirteen, was sitting in an upright chair beside the table, serious and concerned with the tale. Annie sat beside Nelly on the rug, leaning against her Mam's leg. She had been given a sock and some darning wool, for Mam never liked to see her children idle. But Annie, the carefree younger sister, her lank brown hair almost hiding her face, was winding the wool round Nettle's ears. The little white mongrel dog had wormed her way through the family to the fireside, and now she rolled over to play, getting the wool into a hopeless tangle. Mam sighed, and reached over to take the darning in hand, tapping Annie lightly on the head as her hand passed by. Annie whined and looked sulky, as much like Bushman in the sulks as her thin lips could manage. Bushman, with wide, full lips and heavy chin, was better equipped for sulking. He did it well when the mood took him.

The two small boys, Reuben and Alan, curled up in a narrow space between Bushman's rocking chair and the fender, were throwing a pot marble at each other with increasing noise. Alan, the youngest, was teasing stupid, pale Reuben, and Reuben's dogged pushes against his tormentor became wilder at every throw. At last Bushman, taking note of Mam's warning nod, gave them a rough dig with his boots. In the calm that followed, Nelly led him on to tell of the village itself and its romantic past.

Bushman felt completely at home in Thornton. He knew everyone, and everyone had known him since he was born. He had a strong sense of belonging, that Nelly inherited from him. The pattern of village life had developed around him as he grew. He knew the routine of the farming year among rough hill pastures or rich meadows in the little valleys. He had watched as the quarry beyond Billy-a-Doad's farm, at the other side of Cam Lane, had grown into a jagged, dirty hole cut deep in the ground. Being an odd mixture, not a serious man, but one who liked to read, he had opened the fat brown volume of Thomas Whittaker's *History of Craven* which stood on the shelf in his father's bedroom, and he knew a little of the village past. Suddenly, among rough jokes about lambing, or the antics of his boys, he would drop in an odd historical fact, a memory from his reading.

Whittaker's book gave a picture of the hard past that lay behind peaceful Thornton, for Craven is part of the mountainous heart of Yorkshire, a vast mass of limestone heaped into low grassy hills, covered with screes and exposed beds of broken white limestone. The village of Thornton lies on a watershed at the very southern edge of this area, where a valley forms the dividing line between limestone and dark grey millstone grit. Streams run east and west from the parish until the water which is shed in Thornton may end either in the North Sea or in the Atlantic. Through this valley routes crossed the mountainous centre of the country between the flat, fertile land on either side. Thornton had been a place of passage even in Roman times. Craven was always a rough land, hilly and wet, demanding equivalent toughness from its folk.

The first known settlers, Anglo-Saxons advancing into the hills, named the place Torentun, which means Thorn Tree

Farm, and they named the surrounding settlements as well; Elslack, which is Ella's slack or hollow, and Barnoldswick, which is Bernulf's Village. Driving their cattle, laden with household goods, they would find, as they came up the valley from the east, a low green sheltered hill, facing south, one of the few stopping places between the mountains on either side, above the valley marshes and yet below the windy crest. The first camp, by a thorn tree, they called Thorn Tree Farm.

This is all conjecture, for no written story of the time remains; it must be pieced together from names and places, from pieces of information about the land and the crops and the time of year. After three hundred years we have a little writing, mostly chronicles of disaster, for no record of the good times was thought necessary, when men slaughtered their cattle at Michaelmas, ate good roast meat and brewed their own beer to drink outside their homes, or celebrated the new spring in May-time dances around their huts. Thornton was not an easy place to live in. Monks recorded that grain would not ripen properly in the rainy climate of the valleys. Rough bread, a mixture of barley and rye, was made by the people, but most of the land was only fit for growing grass; high, exposed moor for the sheep rather than valley meadows for cattle.

The chronicles of disaster mention two exceptional troubles. First of all, when the north of England rose against William the Conqueror and he laid the countryside waste, it is recorded that in Yorkshire the whole county was left with not more than three thousand folk, perhaps as many as lived in the parish of Thornton, including the mill town of Earby, in Bushman's day. In William's reign the whole of Craven was worth so little that it was let to one Ilbert de Lacey for a rent of five marks and a hawk a year. People returned to Craven slowly and the area began to recover. Of this we know a little from tax returns and the rents that lords drew from their land.

Less than a hundred years later Craven was devastated once again. King David of Scotland marched into Yorkshire with his men, killing all who resisted, driving columns of women and children back to slavery. He felt no regret for the death and misery his men had caused, only pious horror over a few desecrated churches. King David sent back silver chalices to each sacked church out of the loot and spoils of his war. The people returned more gradually.

Again a slow growth followed; a rise from desolation towards prosperity began; but the north was generally at least a hundred years behind the prosperous south, and areas like Craven were behind even the rest of the north. Much of the land was wild and open. Fountains Abbey had a hundred square miles of sheep ranches up on the fells behind Thornton, where the land was occupied by little except a few shepherds and countless sheep. But in time the ordinary folk, the medium-sized farmers, came to prosper, and built themselves scattered farms among their lands.

The farms of Thornton, half a dozen or more, are spread out at intervals along the road leading from Skipton, through the valley, towards Earby and Barnoldswick. Each of them backs on to its fields, and behind are the old stone barns and shippons, beside them one or two cottages for farm workers. These were the essential beginnings of the village, these and the church, although the village never gathered around the walls of its church in the way of a rich lowland parish with its tightly packed cottages. Among hills and fells, where men walked miles along green paths to their worship, the churches were built at natural meeting places, outside any village if none within were well-enough placed. Those ancient paths converge on Thornton church from all the scattered settlements and farms of its wide parish.

During the seventeenth and eighteenth centuries the rough thatched cottages were replaced by solid stone houses of local weavers, who spread their drying cloth like white flags across the countryside behind them. For industry had

15

come, and the village was no longer solely a small cluster of agricultural farms straggling along the road. Small settlements in the valleys, Earby and Barnoldswick, quickly grew into textile towns, sprouting black saw-edged mills, tall chimneys, and rows of stone cottages for the workers.

Bushman could speak of such things from his own experience and Nelly spent a whole childhood of winters beside the fire listening to his tales. She listened well and quietly, felt for the people she heard about and their long-resolved problems. In time she caught elements of her Mam's history and was able to piece the whole story together. Bushman's past linked him closely to Thornton through her Grandad and Grandmother who lived in the Post Office, but Mam came from the sea.

When the tales were over for that night and the children were sent off to the stairs, candlesticks in their hands, Bushman winked at them across the table. 'When I married your Mam I was right let down.' 'What for, Dad?' 'I thought, when her name were Sarah Land, she must own some.' They laughed and chased up the stairs. Nelly and Annie disappeared into the small back bedroom. The boys jumped on to their brass bed in the big, upstairs, front room. It took two at the head and one at the foot and, stripped to their long-tailed shirts, they prepared for the night. Nelly and Annie whispered quietly together in the darkness before they closed their eyes, ready to fall asleep and dream of the stories they had been told. Then Nelly, in sudden recollection of the pig, its staring eyes and bloody tongue, clutched Annie's hand, burrowed down into the soft feather mattress, and pulled the bolster over her head for safety.

Downstairs in the kitchen a sudden bang and muffled laughing disturbed Sarah and the cat. 'It's our Alan, I'll be bound,' she said, for Alan was the youngest, smallest, toughest and most adventurous. Bushman jumped up, opened the door, and stood at the foot of the stairs. 'Jack, Reuben, Alan; who wants a taste of t'stick?' Everything was silent at once; and Bushman, grinning to himself, sat down in the rocking chair again and picked up his newspaper, the *Craven Herald and Pioneer*. Five minutes later, when he looked over the top, Sarah's eyes were closed. He laid the paper flat beside the lamp and turned to the racing page, oblivious to the gusts of driven rain beating against the window.

'Bedtime,' said Sarah when her eyes blinked open after an hour or so, and she got to her feet. The black cat woke up in a flash, shot to the floor, up to the bedroom, on to the pillow and buried itself deep under the bedclothes. They lit a candle and creaked up the stairs, peeping in at the back bedroom where Annie and Nelly lay asleep under the patch-work quilt, its colours of red, white and blue just visible in the flickering light. It had first hung as a flag outside the door for the Queen's Golden Jubilee. In the crowded front bedroom a huddle of boys could just be seen against the far wall by the fireplace. As Sarah and Bushman got into bed they could hear the gentle sound of their children, breathing and turning in their sleep.

2

Sarah's Story

Nelly's mother came into Craven from the east. She came to work, to suffer a private tragedy, and at last to settle in that cottage beside the love tree, where Nelly would be born. Alone, sitting gravely in a red railway carriage, smoothing down her dress and brushing back her hair as the train drew into each station, Sarah Land travelled throughout an autumn day into the rough centre of Yorkshire. She brought determination with her, mixed with a little anxiety, though at twenty-five she had learnt to face a hard world calmly. She also brought a bag and a hat-box, but she wore her Sunday dress and shoes, for they travelled better that way. She had a strong, white face, dark hair and hazel-green eyes, but her chief attraction came from the contrast between her habitual serious smile and the happiness she showed with children and animals.

A painted sign, 'Thornton-in-Craven', swung below the fretted canopy of a tiny, gothic style, railway station. Sarah stepped down from the carriage and lifted out her bags. She could see nothing of the village and seemed to be in the middle of empty countryside, rough and green, full of half-naked trees. Hills rose up all around her. A carrier's cart stood waiting at the end of the platform and she arranged to be taken to the village, 'Aye, it's right up t'hill,' the carrier said. Even the language sounded rougher to her ears. 'Is't thy first time i'Craven, luv?' he said, whipping his horse as it heaved up a steep, tree-lined hill; 'Nay, it's not far to Thornton.' At last a few stone roofs began to appear on the hillside above them, held down against the wind by heavy stone slabs, smoke rising from all the stubby chimneys. The horse staggered over the top of the hill on to a wide level area of gravel. In front of them stood a fully grown lime tree with a worn stone seat like a millstone fixed round its base. 'That's called t'love tree,' said the carrier, then added hurriedly, to forestall the inevitable question, 'nay, but I don't know why.'

The sombre stone village was all round her now, wild enough in the autumn wind for a stranger from the flat coastlands. Sarah sat quietly on her seat as the carrier raised his whip to a group of men in heavy working clothes who stood beside the tree. Rows of dark grey cottages, the stone smooth only round doors and windows, framed the gravel space beside the tree. Beyond it Sarah could just see the village shop and Post Office. The green hill rose up again behind those houses to a low summit which sheltered the village from the worst of the wind.

Fallen leaves blew about the cart wheels. The carter jumped down, poked his head round the Post Office door, and returned quickly. 'Nowt for me,' he said as he clambered up; 'old Mrs Riley at the shop's got a sharp tongue today.' He swung the cart round to follow the road which cut diagonally up the side of the hill. On either side of it more grey stone cottages, some with large weavers' windows, stood in little rows or were notched into corners of the hillside along small muddy lanes. They reached the end of the hill, right in front of a great black Victorian mansion. 'That were built by our Billycock,' said the carter, 'Billycock Bracewell.' 'Oh,' said Sarah, 'I'm going to work for Mrs Bracewell.' 'Aye, well they don't live there now. He's moved on. I'll take thee to Newfield Edge.'

She looked back down the length of this straggling grey village. There could only be a couple of hundred people in those few houses. They must be country people, for farms and outbuildings stood between the cottages. Fingers of fields ran down from the hills right to the back doors. She had travelled only a day's journey from a great port and now she felt back in a more primitive past. Still, in 1875, when Queen Victoria had been almost forty years on the throne, even rough Craven should offer a decent living.

Sarah thought of the family she had left behind, of father and mother, and her big boisterous brothers, fresh-faced from their work at sea, crowding the dockside terraced house in Hull. She thought of the town, the flat land around it, the seaside and the masts of ships which filled the harbour. Hull was a man's town, with not enough work for women, save in the fish sheds. But here in the west were great textile factories crying out for female labour, and prosperous mill-owners crying out for the servants who had gone into their mills for money. Her family could not afford to let her stay idle, even if she had wanted it herself. Purely by chance, in the dense columns of the *Craven Herald*, they found a job for Sarah. It could have been anywhere within a wide region, but in fact the work lay not four miles from Thornton-in-Craven. In her best dress, all prepared, they packed her off into the unknown.

Sarah's adventure into the hills led her to work as cook in Billycock Bracewell's new house. There she joined in all the talk, the fun and the drudgery of work in the kitchen and servants' hall, taking her own chair at the far end of the scrubbed kitchen table. Gaiety, excitement, even licence, came every week for two hours on Wednesday evenings. Then, and then only, young men were allowed into the house, and one by one they carried off the young women, until Mrs Bracewell began to regret her kindness.

So it was on a Wednesday evening that Sarah was first introduced to the housekeeper's younger brother, one William Riley, who arrived, typically enough, with the fine weather. He had lost his original name, for everyone called him Bushman. Sarah asked why and was told, in the teasing spirit of those Wednesday evenings, 'It's that tangle like a hawthorn bush under his nose.' So Bushman, still young and vain enough, laughed an embarrassed laugh and stroked his newly grown moustache, which was certainly fine and bushy, with his strong hands. It took Sarah several months to discover the true reason for Bushman's name.

Bushman brought a friend with him from Thornton, Harry Bell, and soon it became customary for them to tramp four miles over the hills on Wednesdays as the long summer evenings gave time. They would appear round the corner of the dairy, past the great rounded arch of the stable door, Bushman with his jacket over his shoulder, Harry Bell in full waistcoat, his face washed clean of quarry dust. Low evening sun shone on to the flags outside the kitchen door, giving golden faces to the cook, the housekeeper and the maids, creating vast opportunities for banter and flattery when Bushman and Harry, in their dusty boots, came suddenly out of the stable shadow.

Bushman flirted with Mrs Bracewell's lady's maid and, typically, he was so easy with her that she alone escaped those dangerous evenings and went away unmarried. Harry Bell, with his round face free from moustaches, kindly, smiling and reliable, could safely take life more seriously. He and Sarah sat next to each other on the kitchen chairs and then, perhaps because they were both serious-minded folk, perhaps because the kitchen cat climbed laboriously from Sarah's lap and perched on Harry's shoulder, licking the oil in his hair, they smiled a shared happiness. Then, Wednesdays were not merely a general pleasure, but the delight of waiting for a person, who was sure to come. Harry Bell walked over from Thornton on days when Bushman refused to leave the fireside. Sarah rewarded his honest devotion. They married in the spring and rented as their first home the small end cottage beside the love tree in Thornton.

In those days village folk were known by their trade. Farm

labourers, weavers and mill workers, domestic servants or quarrymen, they could all manage to live decently, even if that meant constant care and saving. Everyone had a good vegetable garden, and farms nearby for butter, eggs, milk and perhaps a side of bacon. Some trades, and the quarry work in particular, were seasonal. The men had to find other jobs in bad winter weather when the rock faces were icy or heavy rain began to fill the quarry bottom. There was mild little John Riley, who worked alongside Harry Bell and was no relation to Bushman. He used to travel through the hill villages and mill towns in winter selling cheap Bibles. He was driven harder than most, for his wife was half-way towards the tally of twelve children who would crowd their three-bedroomed cottage for years to come. Somehow John and his wife kept their family on a quarryman's wage. All the children were decently dressed, even if their clothes were showing wear by the time they reached the youngest. Their leather clogs, passed from foot to foot, survived all twelve and were still sound enough to be sold second-hand. John Riley had a large garden. His youngest daughter, fair haired Mabel, became Nelly's best friend at school.

Two or three times that first year Sarah took the train back down the valley to Skipton market. Winter prices were not too bad, with eggs at sixteen for a shilling, beef nine-pence a pound and chickens at five shillings a pair. Harry generally brought in over fifteen shillings a week and Thornton prices were sometimes a little lower than at the market. Sarah earned some extra by dressmaking and so they lived pretty well. Not that quarrymen's families were anything but working folk. Harry and Sarah managed with care, furnishing their house with a few wooden chairs and a table to stand on a well-swept stone floor. When they could afford a roast, and had no means to carve it, Mrs Hartley let them into the secret of the communal carving-knife, hidden in a slit of the love tree and used by all the neighbours. Roasts were not so frequent that they needed one apiece.

Sarah found that she took no time at all to settle in Thornton. With the house to whitewash inside, furniture to be scraped together, some of it remnants left over by Harry's parents when they retired from Bell's Farm, and work to find as a dressmaker, she wasted little time in gossip with the neighbours. She was happy to be quietly about her business, planning and saving, learning the pleasures, and hardships, of a country village. Sarah's family had moved to Hull before she was born, but all her ancestors had been country folk. To live in Thornton was like the return of a desert explorer to his green home, almost a recovery of a lost childhood.

She rescued a black kitten, and raised it to be a big, imperious cat, never happier than when sitting on Sarah or her work. The cat would follow her everywhere with dog-like devotion, and Sarah, with her quiet but determined ways, might have been suspect as a witch if she had lived two hundred years earlier. Only her light, thin voice as she summoned the nameless cat, 'Puss, puss,' revealed the normal human uncertainty behind her calm expression, showing that her silence was half shyness. The rich and rewarding smile which greeted Harry, when he returned home, was another revelation.

Secure in her own home, with a husband who was strong, cheerful and reliable, a solid figure to lean against, once he had changed from his dusty working clothes, Sarah smiled often and even laughed now and then. She invented pleasant little ways of living, and on fine mornings would take bread and cheese for her lunch up to the hilltop behind the cottages. Sitting on the vantage point of a cool stone stile, she could see all the riches of her small world spread below her.

Thornton straggled like a thin grey spider, flattened diagonally across the green hillside. At the spider's head, on the summit of the hill, where the road divided to disappear into the valleys towards Earby and Barnoldswick and their constant grey smoke cloud, stood Billycock Bracewell's house. Down Thornton hill came the main body of that village, an inner row of farms and cottages, among them the school, men's club and forge, protected by an outer hedge of trees as far as the denser cluster of grey buildings around the Post Office. Sarah could see folk crossing the road and groups of children playing in the gravel where the road levelled out and widened beside the love tree. She sighed, smiled contentedly, and hugged her knees together. 'Isn't it grand,' she whispered to the cat, who was sitting close against her on a carefully selected concave stone.

The heart of the village, or perhaps its stomach if the two can be separated, was at her feet, and then the hillside sloped steeply down to the railway line and Elslack beck in the valley bottom. 'No wonder I couldn't see t'village when I arrived,' she thought, and chuckled at her past perplexity. The main road, carrying on its regular course beyond the Post Office, led diagonally down the hill to Skipton and its market place, after passing Fence End House where Mrs Smith lived, landlord to Sarah and most of the village beside. Other little roads and lanes, like the spider's grey legs, branched off into the hillside.

Sarah's thoughts were disturbed by a rustle in the grass below her. She peered attentively until she could see, running towards her, a large glossy blackbird. She put a restraining hand on the cat as the bird stopped below, cocked its head, and opened its bright yellow beak as if to speak. Sarah chirruped softly, and the bird's yellow rimmed eye looked full at her, in apparent understanding. Then the blackbird hopped away along the wall edge. Sarah, in sympathy and interest, got down from her perch and followed it until it disappeared into a hedgerow.

Now she was almost at Cam Lane, and could follow its gravel surface down to the main road. But beyond, cut into the top of Thornton's long hill, at the other end from the black mansion house, she could see dust rising from the quarry, where Harry worked. 'Perhaps I'll go and look over the edge,' she thought. Then she worried whether it might be safe, or wise to do so. She did not much like the quarry. So she turned aside into the meadow and picked a handful of flowers, cowslips, mayflowers, tall green cow-parsley, even buttercups and dandelions. It was a child's posy, to be taken home in delight and carefully placed, without arrangement, in a cracked cup on the kitchen table. Sarah felt she carried summer into the whitewashed house when she returned.

Soon the young Bell's were not thought a newly married couple at all, and then it became evident to the neighbouring wives that they were about to acquire a family. Sarah told no one until the fact was self-evident. She still saw Harry off to the quarry at dawn in winter, and then at six o'clock as the days lengthened into summer. Harry would trudge up a narrow cart track between trees to the stone quarry hut. He collected his pick and, high on the rock, worked at the shattered beds of limestone or shovelled the smaller stuff into trucks on the quarry railway. With the other men he would leave the quarry through its tunnel when the whistle blew and the red flag was raised, to wait for red-headed Shot to fire his charges. Then Mr Bond or Mr Nightingale, the quarry owners, would send them back to a fresh heap of rock ready to be broken into road-stone. As Harry worked in the quarry, Sarah toiled at her dressmaking beside the cottage window.

Shortly after lunch one day, when Sarah looked out and blinked at bright sunlight falling through the love tree's branches, she noticed at the wall corner a dark group of men, tight together, and led by Mr Nightingale. 'I wonder what they're doing there,' she thought, and turned back to her sewing, intending to ask Harry that evening. As she raised her head again she saw the group draw nearer, growing larger and darker against the sunlight as it approached her own door. She got up, and reached the threshold just as Mr Nightingale, with a sideways glance at his men, was lifting a hand to knock.

The image of that black group, the dusty jackets hanging

baggily behind Mr Nightingale's sleek hair, fixed in Sarah's mind and remained there long after their words were forgotten. Mr Nightingale spoke first in his odd, precise, formal way, which made his message seem even more unreal. Beside him she saw the anxious face of John Riley, stone dust marking out the wrinkles. Harry's rougher mates stood sheepishly behind, looking at each other, at the stony ground or the house windows, anywhere rather than at Sarah. Barrell Bradley's great belly projected beyond Mr Nightingale's left elbow. His red face was angled towards his clogs, he blew out his cheeks, held in his hollow voice, and showed his feelings, as usual, through his beefy hands, tapping them uncertainly against his coarse trousers. Two or three other men sheltered behind Barrell's bulk and Sarah noticed half of Shot's head, dusty red against the trees in the valley. At the very rear, a little apart from the rest, stood John James Brown, a big, ugly, single man who cared nothing for other folk's feelings, looking relentlessly sullen, with staring eye and a heavy mouth in his flabby, pale face. As he scuffled his clogs Sarah could see, and always remembered, below his short trousers, the incredible knotted, lumpy, hairy remains of his dark grey socks.

Mr Nightingale finished speaking; John James drifted away at once and the others followed. Sarah stood for a moment on the threshold as the group broke apart, leaving only its impression on her mind. The sun shone full on her out of a beautiful clear sky. 'It can't be true,' she thought, and meant that it mustn't be true. Her mind, accustomed to small plans and large security, raced round in impossible conjectures. 'I'll kill myself,' she muttered, then opened her eyes to find herself staring at rough, varnished wood in the back of the door. 'What shall I do?' she said aloud, turning to the cat for a little comfort, and began to cry at last.

They had broken the news to her as gently as such rough men could. Harry had been working on the steep side of the rock face, where contorted planes run smoothly down to a scree of cuttings below. They were not blasting that day, but loading trucks of broken limestone to be sent down to the railway in the valley. Trucks rumbled steadily along the line, filled with tons of stone, and Harry Bell worked steadily preparing the face for the next day's charges. He slipped, no one knew how or why, and went skidding helplessly down the rocks until he rolled and tumbled over loose stones on to the railway track below. A fully-laden truck was thundering along. Nothing could be done, no one could stop it. No one could pull him clear. Harry Bell was crushed and killed.

The news spread rapidly through the village, and soon neighbours came to sit with Sarah and do their poor best to comfort her. Mrs Riley was always the first to know, and Lizzie Riley, white and ample, was sent round from the shop as soon as her mother heard of the accident. Mrs Hartley from her cottage across the yard came close at her heels, sailing in as always, puffed out like a pouter pigeon. They took control, made tea, expressed sideways sympathy at the 'poor lass with her baby due any time'. But the old rivalries arose even over a kindness, and Mrs Hartley, with beads of sweat in her moustache, said gruffly, 'I expect your mother'll be needing you back at the shop soon, Lizzie Riley.' Lizzie replied fiercely, her spade chin jutting forward, 'I'm sure your family can manage without you for longer, Mrs Hartley.' Then Sarah wanted to jump and scream at them both. But she sat with glazed eyes, her mind running round and round: 'I wish they'd go away.'

Even old Peggy Stockdale from next door poked her scrawny neck round the corner, shook her thin, tangled hair and hissed at Sarah. 'Nay, lass, don't tha take on so,' said Peggy and scuttled away. But she was back in a few minutes, like a tortoise from its shell, to say, 'They've got t'coffin going, cans't hear t'saw?' Sure enough, the sound of Bushman Riley getting down to a rush job came with painful clarity from the open workshop at the yard end.

Sarah could take it no longer. She stood up and made for

the stairs, brushing aside offers of help and supporting hands. As she fell down on the bed her first thought was a sudden, deep hate for Harry, who had left her like this. Then, as her mind began to try and think ahead, as she realized how much of a burden her baby would be, she sobbed slowly into her pillow. Suddenly the cat appeared beside her face, purring for attention. She brushed it roughly on to the floor. 'Whatever shall I do?' she thought. 'What shall I do?'

3

To the Strid

Bushman Riley, the craftsman, sportsman, who delighted in braided coats and fine gestures, who oiled his moustache and went off to the races, was a native of Thornton, his roots deep in the village. While his father's father had been postmaster in the days when the cottages were thatched with straw, his mother's folk had lived just across the road from the Post Office, at the very top of Station Hill, when it was called Booth Bridge Lane, before railway and station were built. There they had run a small shop. Bushman grew up under the combined roof of Post Office and shop, for the two were incorporated in the persons of his father, John Cowgill Riley and his mother, Hannah Riley.

His mother, the matriarch, would sit sternly in the kitchen behind the shop, sheltered by a curtain from draughts and stray, intruding eyes, keeping guard over her treasures. When the shop bell rang she would march out in her black bustle, black shawl and black lace cap, chin pushed forward, bright eyes quick and watchful, to stand behind the dark-stained counter. A great wooden dresser filled the back wall, loaded with deep drawers full of raisins and nuts and grains of rice. There were hessian bags of flour and corn on the floor, and a tin jug full of treacle, its paint a scratched and faded green.

Bushman, when still in his baby skirts, had discovered the treacle jug and found that a rich dark drop sometimes hung on the end of the spout. If his mother's head was turned, he could reach out a quick finger and carry the sweetness secretly to his mouth. But then he risked her wrath. 'What's that dratted lad doing? Will! Come here!' A rap on his head would follow, and young Bushman was sent, tearfully, out into the back yard. The shop, half in darkness, full of smells and sweetness, had all the romance and attraction of a treasure cave for a small boy, even if at times it seemed to be guarded by a dragon.

On the counter stood the round ropes of twist tobacco which Wright-Jack smoked on weekdays, and the knife, honed regularly on the workshop grindstone, which Hannah used to pare off delicate shavings of the strange smelling substance. Some old men chewed it and spat out viscous brown gobs against the love tree stone as they passed. At the other end, out of reach of children's hands, stood slabs of chocolate and toffee and the glass jars of coloured sweets.

Bushman's father, the village postmaster, wheelwright, carpenter and coffin-maker, was called Wright-Jack in due recognition of the importance of the wheelwright to a farming community. Wright-Jack had been recommended postmaster in succession to his father by both rector and landlord. He walked miles each day in all weathers, his bamboo cane in his hand, his long legs moving easily over rough tracks and steep hill paths. Like the prophet descending with his tablets from the mountain, he would return at lunchtime, cool and ready for the rest of the day's work. He would smooth his silky white beard and sit beside Hannah in the back room, passing on the gossip of the village with a dry wit and a biblical sense of propriety.

The work of village craftsman filled Wright-Jack's long afternoons and evenings. He was always busy, and trained Bushman to be his help and successor as soon as the lad could hold a hammer, though he could never instil a sense of responsibility into the boy. Bushman's by-name followed in due course, as he learnt to make the central bushes of wheels in grey-brown elm. Through years in the workshop he was initiated into all the technical details of his craft, the properties of the different woods, the correct use of tools, the various joints, their strengths and weaknesses, and the finer skills of finish and decoration. In time he had his own particular methods, his delicate work with adze and chamfering plane and his liking for well-smoothed timber.

Bushman loved making coffins. He himself never said why, perhaps because it was no mere repair job, but a complete work of his own skill, whether in deal, elm or oak, according to the taste and wealth of the dead man's family. Wright-Jack had taken him along as soon as he was old enough to be useful. 'I were only thirteen when me Dad took me to measure Bert Robinson,' he would boast at the pub for years to come. 'Cans't remember old red-faced Bert? He died suddenly on a hot day, on his way to t'quarry, and his knees were all drawn into his stomach.'

Wright-Jack had led Bushman into the Robinsons' front room, and inspected the corpse in a businesslike way. The legs still bent sharply, knees in the air. 'Will! Hold t'legs,' said his father efficiently, and walked round to put his weight on the shoulder, for a corpse had to be straight in the coffin. Bushman was keen to help, and he pressed down the legs with enthusiasm, being careful to level the knee joints. Then he turned towards his father at the top of the table for approval. But he had been too quick for both Wright-Jack and the stiff joints of the dead man. There, sitting bolt upright on the table, staring him straight in the eye, was the blank corpse, lolling its open jaw at him. 'I thought old Bert were coming to take me with him,' Bushman would say.

He let go at once and jumped back against the wall, as the corpse fell slowly down on his waiting father. Wright-Jack, though accustomed to the odd ways of corpses, felt a moment's doubt at this sign of life. The two of them stood blinking at each other from the corners of the room as Bert

Robinson lay quiet, his knees still in the air. Then his father's laughter brought a forced grin to Bushman's sheepish face. After that introduction the business never worried him. In the workshop he would labour cheerfully on the coffins, planing timbers, making shallow saw cuts so that they would bend to shape. Finally he would stand back, look at his work, go into the house and say, 'Let's have a pillow to try, mother, I do like to see them comfortable.'

So Bushman was born into three prosperous inheritances, heir to the Post Office, to the shop and to the wheelwright and joinery business. In addition he benefited from the seasonal use of the house by shooting gentlemen; Mr Watkinson, a manufacturer from Huddersfield, and his friends regularly came to stay at weekends in autumn. They brought with them their own maid, occupying the three best bedrooms and their maid a closet between them. Bushman's mother and father, he and his sister, moved out into the back bedroom or with neighbours, and the gentlemen took over the house. They ate in the best front-room, they had bath water brought every evening. Full hot baths were carried up laboriously in pails, carried down again by the women of the household, to be emptied into the gutter in the back yard. But Mr Watkinson and his friends lived well and paid well. They had their soup, roast, and apple pies for dinner. They expected to be provided with hot freshly-baked pasties to take out with them after breakfast, and Bushman's mother rose at six in the morning to make them. Bushman lived well on the profits of all this industry.

Thornton Post Office was a fine square stone house in the centre of the village, with a pediment over the door and a small flower garden in front. Bushman was educated to suit his expectations. He had been sent away to school at Rawden College over by Leeds to get good, sound, Quaker knowledge. He knew the Bible by heart. He was a reading man like his father, and when he held a leather-bound book

32

in his hands his voice would take on a different flavour, half way to gentility.

For Bushman himself was the youngest son and the favourite. Most of his brothers and sisters had married and left. Only the spoilt younger children remained, Bushman and Lizzie. Lizzie was like the other girls, with the dark hair, square chin, white face and heavy build, always ready to take charge of things, to rule the roost. And Bushman was brought up to expect that all he saw around him would one day be his.

Sarah next door made his clothes, and she had begun to train young Lizzie as a dressmaker. Bushman had a best suit with braided lapels and beautifully-buttoned waistcoats. Most significantly of all he, as his father did, wore boots and not clogs, except of course when going about heavy work in the garden. Ordinary folk, mill folk, farm labourers, men, women and children, all wore solid black leather clogs with heavy iron plates fixed to the wooden soles for long life. Boots were for those, like Bushman, who had an independent position in the village.

The clatter of clogs across the back yard to the privy was an early morning serenade for any late sleeper near the Post Office. Sarah herself, after four years in Thornton, was quite at home with clogs. They slipped easily on her cold feet one morning as she crossed the yard to the privy, their iron sole-plates ringing against frost-coated stone slabs. The last three years, since Harry died, had been a time of scraping and care. Baby Jack was born, and he added to her insecurity, even if thought and love for her baby filled some of the emptiness in her life. Responsibility, work, rent to pay, food to prepare, with only herself to rely on, were all accepted by Sarah with the ruthless logic of survival: 'You can't afford to be soft.' That became clear to her in the long nights of dressmaking, when she learnt the value of glycerine and hot water for her tired eyes.

Sarah peered round the icy edge of the privy door and saw

33

Bushman Riley standing in sunlight beside the workshop, his waistcoat buttoned against the cold, but with no collar on his striped flannel shirt. He held a great black pair of iron calipers in his hand. They were big competent hands, well cared for like his tools, washed clean before every meal and very rarely marked by clumsy cuts with an adze, even after the morning's work following a late night at cards. He was looking at a broken cart shaft, piecing it together in his mind with some length of wood stored in the loft above. His eyes were not stubborn, or mischievous, as they could be, but brown and thoughtful. He blew out a cloud of breath through his heavy moustache and put his hand to his plump chin in thought.

As she shivered in the privy Sarah still had that sunlit image in her mind. Bushman had a good body, and Sarah, when she made his braided jacket, had fitted it closely to the strong shoulders. He was sleeker, less dusty, than Harry Bell had been, though she carefully avoided the comparison. He watched her about the yard, just as she watched him at work.

Bushman often brought round spare vegetables, saying that his mother had told him to bring them. He helped her to carry heavy loads of coal into the house and got his thanks for it. Sometimes he got less kind words when he drove carts or wagons past her clean washing as it hung across the yard, but he had to accept his due.

The yard, its slabs of stone and chippings, corners green with weeds and little hiding places behind the closet walls, had been young Bushman's playground and now he saw Jack busy in the same great work of exploration. When Jack came too close to his saw, or picked up shining chisels, Bushman would say 'Now, lad,' and carry him across to Sarah, shaking the wood-shavings from him as they went. More and more frequently on such occasions he could be tempted to stay for a cup of tea. Wright-Jack's sarcasm, the remarks about 'Stopping work every five minutes', were not enough to save him from himself. For Sarah, unlike the women in his own family, would listen with interest to his tales.

Sarah sat down, rubbed her eyes, and looked from the material in front of her to three-year-old Jack playing with his pile of clippings on the floor. Bushman had been good with Jack, for he was a favourite of all the children about the yard, played with them, talked to them, and liked to hold them on his knee and tell them stories. Last summer he had brought round a basket of new peas from his garden and put them down on the table, calling young Jack over to help him shell them. He began to show Jack how to do it and Sarah went out of the room for a moment until she heard a chuckling and then Bushman's voice sounding a warning. 'Now then, young Jack,' he said, 'you start whistling.' So Sarah popped her head round the door and said, 'Why should he whistle?' To which Bushman replied, 'Well, if I can hear him whistling, then I know that t'peas are going into t'pan and not into his mouth.' So Sarah laughed, and Bushman laughed, and Jack, who could neither whistle nor understand much beyond the happy good humour of the occasion, laughed in sympathy.

Three years of close observation gave Sarah some understanding of Bushman's pleasant but pleasure-loving ways. When shouts rather than clogs woke her early one Saturday she pulled the curtain aside to look out of the bedroom window, through the half-leafed love tree, at the noisy folk outside. Bushman was there jumping, with both feet together, up and down from the love tree seat, proving his fitness, trying not to breathe too much steam into the cold air, as his watch chain bounced at every movement and glinted in the low spring sunlight. Barrell Bradley, the stout pig-headed quarryman, stood beside him, not deigning to compete, but looking solidly up the road rather than at Bushman.

He turned his head slowly at a movement half-way up the

village. Hartley Procter, Bushman's limping bad-example, to whom Hannah Riley would never speak, believing that he led her son astray, shambled out of his door and slammed it behind him. In his awkward, loose-limbed way, he came down the hill, swinging a riding crop at tall plants as he passed. The riding crop was fine, leather-covered, silver handle slightly dented, and it came from his wife's family. Hartley Procter was dressed in his best, to suit a working farmer out for the day. His jacket fitted loosely, he wore a waistcoat, but refused to button it. Stringy neck and the lump of an adam's apple were displayed by his open collar. Hartley Procter wandered up to Bushman, grabbed his arm in mid jump, and pulled him into full sunlight to study his appearance. 'Bloody hell, Bushman, are t'going to a wedding?' said Hartley Procter.

Bushman was spared further embarrassment by the appointed arrival of William Edmonson's cart coming up from the Old Road. William was a kindly man, a proper farmer, bearded, thin and tall, never ailing, active and cheerful; with no sons of his own he could never resist a chance to give pleasure to other people's. He drew his horse in beside the love tree and raised his whip in greeting. 'Billy-a-Doad's not here; sleeping as usual,' said Hartley Procter. 'Nay, he's not,' came a light voice from behind the love tree, and as they turned, its owner stepped, equally lightly, round the stone seat. Billy-a-Doad's ruddy face beamed even at Hartley Procter, his curly black hair already beginning to spring from under his billycock hat. Before anyone could move he had bounced into the front seat beside William Edmonson, leaving the others to clamber into the back of the cart. William cracked the whip once. Bushman and his cronies were off, talking quietly, up Thornton Hill towards a full day at the Gisburn races.

A curtain moved in the Post Office front bedroom as Bushman's watching mother left her post. She distrusted her son's friends and his easy-going nature. Once again she determined that he must be made to get down to steady work. Sarah also left her window and sat down to her sewing, feeling lonely and tired. She heard nothing more that day. Half-way through the night, so it seemed, the sound of shouted good-nights woke her, and she heard Bushman cursing as he tripped in the dark over loose flags on his way through the yard to the back door of the Post Office. She could almost feel the icy, disapproving, silence that met him.

That was a disturbed night for everyone, save Bushman, who had the after effects of a bellyful of ale as a sleeping draught. The yowling and screeching which began in the yard, as a half moon lit the whole hillside village, echoed from stony house fronts until it seemed the space must be full of amorous cats. Windows shot open. Mrs Hartley cursed gruffly from her bedside, while her sickly thin husband wheezed under the clothes. Wright-Jack himself emerged and advanced to his back wall, in nightshirt, Hannah's black cape, and unlaced boots, to hurl billets of wood into the dark corners where unwelcome singers might be hiding. Sarah, knowing that the female cause of all this revelry and indignation sat, purring with self-satisfaction, at the bottom of her bed, put her head under the covers and chuckled until she slept.

Deputations visited her next day, and among them Bushman, as representative of the Post Office's yawning inhabitants. He was yawning himself, white faced, and obviously under a cloud at home, for he stayed for a cup of tea and was most unwilling to leave. Clearly something was on his mind that day, for he had no tales to tell, and they sat through long silences. 'Nay, Sarah,' said Bushman at one point, for he had taken to calling her Sarah, and she did not object. Then after a silence, he said 'Nay, Sarah' again, and reached across the table to take her hand. But he put it down again shortly, looked her in the face almost in desperation and rose to go.

Sarah smiled, but kept silent, content to leave time, his own easy inclinations, and the pressure of his parents' strictness, to work on Bushman. She liked him well enough, and he could offer good security. But Bushman found his escape in business. 'Dost reckon t'cats'll be back tonight?' 'Better ask her,' said Sarah, nodding at the black cat on the windowsill. Then she added, 'Tha could help me, Bushman.' 'Aye,' he replied without much conviction. 'Put her in t'coal box this evening, that'll keep her quiet.' Bushman's second 'Aye' was said on the doorstep, as he set off unhappily homewards.

The black cat brought them together at last. Bushman strode jauntily into Sarah's kitchen next morning and announced, 'I've news for thee. Your old cat's had her husband with her all night. I opened t'door just now, and they both shot out, right between my legs.' He made an owlish, amazed face and jumped back in mock surprise. Sarah chuckled good-humouredly at him, and he grinned in reply. Then full of courage, and inspired by the cats' example, Bushman advanced towards her and took hold of both hands. He proposed, and Sarah accepted him. When Bushman put his arms round Sarah and pulled her down to sit on his knee, Jack emerged from behind the dollytub so amazed and wide-eyed that they burst out laughing to see him.

Bushman's mother, who was not a mere dragon, but a lady of considerable sense, had always respected Sarah. She accepted her as a woman who would not easily give way to Bushman's whims and spoke with her on equal terms. 'Well, Sarah, our Will has some sense in him I see. You must come in to tea. Here, share this apple with me . . . Do you know, they're fourpence a pound.' That was full, ungrudging acceptance. Sarah recognized it and was grateful. Wright-Jack could charm and be charmed, he was no problem to Sarah. A kiss on the cheek, above the silky beard, and Wright-Jack's simple reply, 'Well, Sarah, may the Lord bless you both.'

Sarah was the one who had doubts, or rather, vague fears

and uncertainties about her own intentions. She had seen too much of life to accept Bushman's romantic nonsense, now that he could freely indulge it. She knew that marriage did not mean living happily ever after. But the day came, and she had no wish to withdraw. She and the cat woke up to summer sunshine and prepared for the work ahead. The well-known ritual carried her through the morning and she smiled beautifully at Bushman when they met beside the altar. They emerged from church a smiling couple.

Wedding breakfast in the Post Office was full of jokes and relations, cold ham, tea, cakes and cream. Then, at last, they were free to spend the whole afternoon and evening on their honeymoon. Bushman helped his Sarah up the steep side of a wagonette on to the slatted wooden seats behind the driver. The man whistled to his horses, cracked his whip, and half the village waved goodbye as they disappeared under the first trees of Thornton Drag, the long slow slope down the valley side. Even a quiet wedding was an event in Thornton. Once under the trees they could see the steep path that ran up the hill to the quarry, and Sarah turned her head away to avoid bad luck and unhappy memories. Bushman, for once, was sensitive to her feelings. He put his arm round her shoulder, and its weight felt reassuring. She could see his cuffs with the silk braid she had sewn on so carefully. When his strong fingers gripped the hollow above her collar-bone she smiled and said, 'Nay, Will.'

Elm, ash and sycamore passed by under Quarry Hill, and they were out in the sunshine. Then, with splendid, slowly changing views, they rolled along green valley roads to the market town of Skipton, into the cobbled market place, past the cross, and up its wide centre towards the imposing castle entrance, its carved motto, 'Desormais', and the steep bailey wall that ran along beside the road. Six miles in an hour and a half, that was good going, and at a steady pace. They climbed into the hills beyond Skipton and then down into the valley of the River Wharfe. The wagon stopped beside the ruins of Bolton Abbey; they clambered down and wandered among its grey stones towards the shallow-running river.

Sarah and Bushman followed the river-bank into the woods where hills began to rise and the river grew narrower. Slippery rocks were undercut by water and the river ran deep with smooth hollows, bubbling and black under the dark trees. In later years by the fireside, Bushman would tell his children the legend of that place just as he had told it to their mother on that sunny day.

Far back in the distant past, so it was said, a young boy, heir to Skipton castle and all its lands, son of the Lady Adeliza de Romille, used to follow the path of the river and leap gaily and perilously across the narrow gap where they now stood. There, at the strid, it was one bold stride for a man over the slippery rocks to cross to the other side. The lad passed over time after time. At first he would run under the shadow of the trees down to the water's edge to prove his courage, but soon it became easy, an ordinary crossing place.

One day he took a young hound on its leash with him. They ran together down the strid and he leapt lightly from the edge. The frightened young dog crouched down, its legs braced and claws scratching on the smooth rock. Stopped in the air, his hand still clutching the leash, the boy fell short. No one would know how his fingers slithered over the smooth rocks, desperately searching for a crevice, just a small patch of roughness which would give a hold. How long did he struggle as the current pulled at his body and his soaked clothing dragged more heavily on his aching arms? The river took hold of him, pulled him under and held him down, until hidden currents released his body into shallower water.

He was found among shingle and waterweeds under the open sky where the Wharfe runs through peaceful meadows. Dragged from the water, his body was carried slowly back to the castle to his waiting mother. In her grief she established the first Abbey at Bolton, by the riverside on those same green water meadows. There monks prayed for the soul of her drowned son, and there they raised church, cloisters, chapter house, dorters, barns and kitchens in grey stone through the centuries.

Bushman and Sarah had wandered among the ruins of that great Abbey, on grassy paths that were once the floors of arched rooms, where prayers echoed eternally to the skies. As they walked Bushman drew out the horrors of the tale with proper relish and then led his wife through the woods towards the strid. Sarah stood by the water's edge peering into its swirling black movement until her head began to spin and she was almost ready to fall. Bushman stood on the other bank and grinned at her. At last, when he gave her a hand to cross, and she stood trembling beside him he burst out laughing. Ever after when they had sharp words, he would say, 'I should have let thee drown,' and Sarah would reply drily, 'Aye, I wish tha had.'

4

A Witch in the Yard

The night following Billy-a-Doad's pig killing which Nelly and her father had attended Sarah sat up in bed thinking about her family. Eleven years after her marriage to Bushman the house seemed full of children. The honeymoon was a distant memory. The candle beside her flickered in the draught from the stairs, and she buttoned her nightdress up to the chin, pulling the bedclothes closely around her. 'Aye, it's wild out,' said Bushman, in between the grunts he always made when tugging off his boots. Branches of the love tree tapped against the window-panes. Reuben, disturbed by the noise, turned over and began to snore, loose cheeked and open-mouthed until Alan, with a skill developed over the years of sleeping three to a bed, opened one bright eye, dug a sharp elbow into Reuben's stomach, and returned to sleep in a satisfactory silence. Sarah looked across at her lads.

'We need to move house, Will. It's getting too tight now they're all growing up.' Bushman grunted from his pillow 'There'll be t'Post Office when Dad retires.' 'We can't wait that long,' said Sarah, and turned fiercely to confront her complacent husband. Then she sighed. His head was almost buried under the clothes, his breathing ostentatiously regular. She must sort it out herself. She blew out the candle and settled down, close against Bushman's warm back.

That was a hard winter, with cold and damp, bitter winds

and long miserable weeks of rain. It brought a great weeding-out of the old and sickly in the village. Mrs Hartley's husband nearly died of asthma with complications, while next door to the Rileys, old John Stockdale was brought to bed at last. He was a stubborn round-shouldered, surly man, who had worked his sixty years and more as a gardener. Most mornings he set off at dawn with his knobbly cane to walk the two miles to the moor's edge where his employer lived. All day he was there, in wind and rain, Monday to Saturday, for his ten shillings a week, and in the evenings, stubborn as ever, he went back down the fellside and up the hill to Thornton.

At last even John Stockdale's stubborn body was exhausted. He crawled to bed with bronchitis and died in two days. Old Peggy, his wife, left alone, with little money for rent, food or anything else, sat beside a tiny fire, in fear of the workhouse.

Nelly, sent next door with a loaf of bread, found old Peggy in her kitchen. She had a short greasy clay pipe in her mouth, her hands were tightly clenched on her knees, and a pot of tea stewed inside the open oven next to the coals. Half the kitchen was taken up by an enormous stone coal box, the rest of it, lit only by the dull fire, had rough walls covered with smoky whitewash under a low, cracked and yellowish ceiling. The stone flags on the floor were black with dirt, except by the fire itself where a spray of fine grey ash spread evenly from the grate across to the rug under Peggy's chair and speckled the front of her clogs. She was staring into the fire when Nelly knocked lightly on the door and came in.

Nelly's timid approach to the fireside, even the child's white hand touching a grubby grey sleeve, had no effect on Peggy. Nelly stood anxiously beside the chair, hands tightly clasped around a large cottage loaf, but determined to carry out her duty. Suddenly, old Peggy jerked her neck and turned. 'Now, then! What dost tha want?' Her wrinkled dirty face peered up at Nelly, with fierce but cloudy eyes.

She hissed out the words through gaps between her stumps of teeth. 'Has't nowhere to go?'

Nelly put her hand to her mouth and stood back from the chair. 'Mrs Stockdale,' she whispered, 'my Mam told me to bring round some bread. She's just baked it.' Old Peggy put a trembling hand to her ear. 'Has't lost tha tongue?' She had obviously heard nothing, and Nelly tried again. 'My Mam sent some bread,' she shouted, clearly and in desperation, hurriedly putting the loaf down on the table.

Peggy pulled herself up on the back of the chair. 'Thy Mam,' she said, 'thy Mam! Sithee, I want nowt from thy Mam! Take it away, Nelly Riley.' And she knocked the loaf on to the floor, where it rolled into the dirt below the table. She was leaning forward, supported on her arms, her breath hissing through her teeth. Nelly, frightened, unable to understand where she was to blame, fled through the door and out into the safety of the yard.

There she began to cry, quietly, without fuss. Once back home she could sob properly, in comfort, into her Mam's apron. Mam looked surprised, for Nelly was generally the capable 'little mother' of the family. 'Why Nelly, whatever's the matter?' And Nelly told her, as much as she could understand. Mam frowned. 'I reckon Peggy Stockdale's not been right in t' head since her John died. But I'll not have her frightening t'lasses,' and she stroked Nelly's long hair reassuringly, with comfort-giving hands. Then, hearing Reuben sniggering to Alan, she said, 'What's that?' 'Old Peggy's a witch, old Peggy's a witch.' Baby Alan repeated in a squeaky sing-song what he had just heard. 'It were Percy Hartley that first said it,' muttered Reuben, defensively. 'Well, I'll have no more of that nonsense,' Mam replied sharply.

She took Nelly's hand, deciding that they all needed to get out. 'Come on, lasses, let's go up to feed t'hens,' said Mam in her light voice. She put on her cape and shooed them out to the workshop. A sack of corn stood by the wall, dusty with firm round seeds which slipped through their fingers. Carrying a half-filled bucket, Mam led the way up the muddy path at the corner of the yard, past the Hartley's house, along the side of a dry-stone wall, into the garden. She sent all the children hunting among the bare gooseberry bushes in search of her pet toad. Alan found him under a clod, small, bright-eyed, sleepily crawling away from them. He was picked up and passed from hand to hand, wetting their warm palms in a desperate effort to make his escape. Annie wouldn't go near him, but Mam stroked his warty back and talked to him in a gentle voice. Then Reuben was told to put him safely back under the dead leaves. Mam had a kindness for all animals. She talked to them and they trusted her, dogs and cats, hens, geese, goats, horses and even toads.

They scrambled over the limestone wall, passing the bucket carefully, clog-irons slipping on the smooth wet stone. The path led up to Wilson's Fold on the top of the low hill above the village. There they could look down on heavy slate roofs, shining wet with the drizzle, the bare trees around the houses, the green valley below and grey-brown fells beyond. But the hens had seen them. There was no time to waste. In front as ever was Mam's favourite blue, the only one among a clutch of common Rhode Island Reds. She was an aristocrat and she knew it. She kept the others at bay until she had a handful of grain from Mam's own hand, and Mam talked to her just as she did to the toad. When she stopped laying Mam wouldn't have her killed and she finally died of old age. Bushman had to bury her secretly in a corner of the field.

Mam led them back down the hill towards home, the empty bucket clanging in her hand. As they rounded the corner into the yard they came suddenly upon old Peggy, bent over her dead husband's stick, hobbling across to the privy. She looked, indeed, like the witch from a story, with her dirty clothes, scraggy hair, deeply wrinkled face and the odd trembling gestures, the muttered phrases as she shuffled about the yard.

She saw them coming, and stopped her slow lurching walk. 'Sithee, Sarah Riley,' she hissed, damp and grey, the drizzle clinging to her hair. 'Keep them cauf-heeds off,' and she nodded viciously at the group of children, the younger ones sheltering behind Mam's skirts. Annie began to howl, and Mam retorted, 'You leave them alone.' But Peggy was rambling mostly to herself, so Mam ushered the children past her and was on her way to the back door. Suddenly Peggy raised her head, yelled 'Witch thi sen!' in a cracked shriek, spat on the ground, and made off at a fast shuffle.

For a day or two Nelly and Annie lived in terror of old Peggy and hardly dared to go into the yard. Then the full story came out. Mrs Hartley was on the doorstep like a heavy black cloud, her own lads sobbing behind her, Reuben and Alan held firmly by an ear apiece. 'I've thrashed my two,' she began, and then explained how she had seen the four of them hiding in the corner behind the privies, waiting for Peggy Stockdale. Half fearfully, half in malice, they had peered round the stones, yelled 'Witch' and thrown handfuls of gravel at the old woman. 'Why, the poor old creature,' Sarah said, and glared at the boys. 'It's a proper thrashing do for you.' She took down Bushman's leather razor strop from its nail above the sinkstone, and sent Nelly across to fetch Bushman himself. His strength would be needed.

Bushman thrashed them well, but that was not enough to make them friends with Peggy again. She refused to speak to anyone and hardly left her kitchen, where she slept in her chair. When she had been a full day without coming out, even to go to the privy, Sarah badgered Bushman and his father into breaking open the door. Sure enough Peggy sat, dead, before the ashes of her fire.

A group of staring, whispering children gathered around the door and edged over the threshold, hoping to see the dead witch. Sarah and Mrs Hartley shooed them roughly away, then went through the house, making a mental inventory of its poor contents. 'We'll lay her out in t'front room, Mrs Riley,' said Mrs Hartley.

Sarah had been thinking about the dead woman's house, for it was larger than her own, and very convenient, being right next door to the Post Office. So she stepped round to have a word with Bushman's mother. 'Aye, it's rented from Mrs Smith like thine and mine, Sarah. Shall I have a word with her?' Grandma Riley was virtually the landlord's agent in the village.

Nelly was astonished and upset when her Mam and Dad began to talk of moving next door. She thought of it as a horrid, dirty cave, still haunted by the harsh old woman she had seen by the fire. She loved her present home, her memories, however short, of living and playing with her sister and brothers. She liked desperately to be settled and for several nights went to bed crying. Her Mam, with plans to make, found this sudden weakness of her elder daughter very irritating, and was sharp with her in consequence. What silly weakness, to worry about old, dead Peggy. What was done, was done. She had negotiated good terms with Mrs Smith, getting the cottage at the same rent as her old one, two shillings a week, because of its condition.

They set to work on improvements, for the Stockdales had lived in a depressingly old-fashioned way. Bushman smashed out the coal box with his hammer and made the back kitchen into a family sized room fitted with a new cast-iron grate and hot-water boiler. He took out the primitive backstone, where cakes had been baked against the fire's heat, and installed an oven in the front room instead. Memories of old Peggy Stockdale began to disappear under new wallpaper and whitewashed ceilings. By late March they were ready.

The family spent a full Saturday moving in furniture. Bedroom windows were opened wide and chests and brass bedsteads swung in from one house to the next. Bushman and Jack, helped by Grandad Wright-Jack, pushed and slid things into their new places. While Mam took charge of the rearrangements the excited children rushed in and out and chattered to each other about every development in their new home.

There it was, Love Tree Cottage, a small stone house hanging against the side of the Post Office: a box of grey stone with a slate roof and two rooms on each floor divided by another stone wall. From the windows or door of the downstairs front room could be seen the valley and the bleak moors beyond. The back door opened out to the yard and its window looked across to the closets, the path to the garden and the sheltering hill behind the village. Hidden under the stairs was a small whitewashed basement larder with stone slab shelves and a little grilled window high on the wall.

Up narrow stairs, the small back room, where the girls could grow up in proper privacy, had just space enough for their big bed with black-painted frame and brass knobs. Once the bed was in, and Dad had reassembled it, Nelly and Annie sat side by side bouncing up and down on the base looking at each other and giggling. When Alan stumbled in he insisted on standing up, holding the bars, and screeching with delight as his feet went through the springs. 'Nelly, Annie, stop that racket.' Mam's voice pierced the floor. She had just come into her new kitchen. 'Ceiling'll come through. Get down here to help carry.'

The helping had its moments, for Mam knew her children's ways. Nelly and Annie were told to take their Christmas dolls round, and when they were laid to sleep on the dresser top inside the door, with a bolster under their heads and floppy feet hanging down the front, the lasses could feel at home in their new room. Then they watched as Bushman took the end frames of his own big bed into the long front room with its two windows. The boys' bed was already up.

The front room downstairs was soon filled by a large square table with stained turned legs, covered with a velvet-pile cloth, where Mam and Aunt Lizzie cut out and made up servants' dresses for the village. Dressmaking, cooking, talking, reading, playing dominoes or the piano, the children grew up as much in that living-room as in the working kitchen. The front room held a large black-leaded cooking range, with coal fire behind iron bars in the middle and closed ovens on either side, heated by the fire. Now Mam could find space for everything, even her dresser with its cut-glass knobs and drawers full of treasures, sealing-wax and seals, keys, brooches, table-cloths and crocheted napkins.

The back room was kitchen and workroom. Mam covered old Peggy's stone-flagged floor with oilcloth. A round table for ordinary meals stood before the fire, the clothes rack above it. No oven this time, but a great black boiler was built around the fire which provided hot water for washing of all kinds. Baths were taken in a tin bath on the hearth, with hot water ladled from the boiler and ladled back out again when the bath was over. Baths were all right in winter when the water tub by the back door was full but in summer the level sank and Mam didn't like to use the water because it was full of little red wriggling creatures. Bushman would have to take a couple of buckets down to the well in the wall and fill them with cold spring water. He objected to doing it and in those times they did without baths or a lot of washing.

5

Bushman's Wheels

Bushman was always busy in the weeks before May Day. It made no difference that they had moved to a new house. The demands of a farming village on its only wheelwrights came fast and heavily when farmers, having let things lie all winter – broken cart sides, rotten spokes, wagons left out in rain and damp since hay-making – suddenly realized, as the spring grass began to grow, that they must have repairs done today. Carts, wagons, wheels and frames collected in odd angles of the yard until Wright-Jack was forced to take time off his postal round and arrange to hire a shed, and Bushman had to knuckle down to long hours of work. After lambing it was time to begin making and mending the shilvins, ladder-like frames for cart ends, which kept sheep and lambs inside during the two-hour drive to Skipton market. Great, high, solid shilvins also gave a wagon room for up to three tons of hay when the time for hay-making came round.

The spring rush was compounded by the usual distractions of spades to haft, wheelbarrows to repair, and penny shuttlecock bats to make in preparation for Easter. Then, on top of it all came the May Day procession, when every wheeled vehicle that could be found was hauled from its resting place in a field corner. Its wheels were quickly smartened up with a coat of good, sticky tar, and it was harnessed to a reluctant and retired horse which had never expected to be placed in such an undignified position again, and showed it quite clearly by the look in its eye.

Living as he did over his workplace, Bushman could use time as it came to him. On cold mornings he would stay inside, ladle hot water from the boiler into a bowl and shave himself at the kitchen table, his sleeves rolled up, as he sharpened the cut-throat razor on the leather strop which hung beside the window. Then he was ready for the workshop. The double doors were open, white light poured in and he had to work to keep himself warm. Even in his stiff, coarse, and heavy suit a man must be active in the cold. But there were odd pleasures saved up for the days when he had time and the inclination to try his skill. The carved end of an old pew, well-finished, ready-squared timber, had been stored in the corner at the back, behind a stack of deal planks from the sawmill. It was a nice bit of timber, ready planed and rubbed down. He brushed it over and blew the dust off his fingers. Then he took down a fine tenon saw and scribed the first cut. Bushman made out of that pew end a little lidded sugar box to hang on the kitchen wall, just to the left of the brass warming pan that Sarah brought with her from Hull.

The stone-flagged floor of the workshop was littered with wood shavings. Like the cottage it was a solid stone box of a building, roofed with great slabs of stone and built to last. Small paned, cobwebby, windows gave a little light to the other side of the bench which stretched the full length of one wall, saw-marked and littered with tools. A great wooden screw-vice rose up towards the end, big enough to hold a cartwheel upright. The tool-rack was hung with chisels and planes, augers, spokeshaves and paring knifes, all well greased and sharpened, ready for use.

Wright-Jack had anchored a great plank to the far wall beside the grindstone, set with square holes which would take hands and feet on the way up to the loft above. Timber for immediate use or for seasoning was stacked away there, brown elm in piles of round logs still in their bark, long blocks of pale ash roughly square, strange bundles of split jagged oak with shakes and waney edges. Bushman and Wright-Jack carried a mental tally of their stocks, could generally match a problem piece at once, and knew from weight, feel and sound whether it could do its particular job.

Bushman's training in craftsmanship was not all spent in the workshop or over corpses. A wheelwright must know his materials as well as his tools. Different trees produced wood for different uses, and some trees were good for nothing. A man must be taught to look. So it was that most winters, when the sap had died well down, Bushman and Wright-Jack set off into Lancashire on a hired cart, empty except for a great two-handed saw and their bundles of clean linen. They travelled over the forest of Bowland into the valley of the little river Hodder and stayed with distant cousins at Whitewell. There they chose their trees and cut them down themselves with the two-handed saw. They walked along hedgerows where the grass was still crisp from the night's frost and looked at elms and ashes planted for just this purpose when the fields were enclosed a hundred years before. Then, with the trees chosen and cut, they arranged for a heavy four-horse wagon to carry the large timbers to the saw mill at Booth Bridge below Thornton. Lighter, more manageable pieces, the bundles of split oak, the straight limbs of ash trees, good for axe handles, were piled into their cart.

Like a moving wood heap, the laden cart would creak back into the yard sometime in February, and Bushman and Wright-Jack would climb down, starved with cold, to a welcoming party of family and neighbours. They would all go into the back room of the Post Office and stretch out at the fireside. Next day was soon enough to begin clearing space in the workshop for the new wood. Before long the spring rush would be on them, capped by a final flurry for May Day, and then a steady flow of repairs would take them through early summer, until the onset of hay-making and full days of work into long light evenings, when night hardly closed down on an urgent job before dawn seemed to be in the sky calling them back to the workshop. But, once that pressure had passed, Bushman's summer season came into its full freedom of cricket, games of knurr and spell when he competed with his mates to see who could strike a stick farthest down the road, trips to the races, even the pleasures of late and leisurely hay-making in evening sunlight.

Summer was still a distant hope when Bushman prepared himself and his tools for the spring rush. Time hung on their hands until Wright-Jack had him sorting the new timber and re-stacking it for better seasoning. Then, suddenly, everyone was on to them at once. At each new arrival Bushman came to the workshop door and stood in the sunshine to see who it was, ran his hands through his hair, fluffed up his moustache and brushed the shavings from his trousers. A line of carts gathered, framed and planked like boats, but with the ribs outside. They were built of solid timber to last a lifetime, oak and elm and beech. Their frames were bevelled and planed for lightness.

Bushman heard an old friend of his when it was brought into the yard at last. Indeed, everyone around heard it as its wheels screeched and groaned on the axle and a tyre rang loose against the felloes of the wheel rim. Bushman had worked time and again to keep William Edmonson's ancient wagon together. Now it was back, like a rheumatic patient at the doctor's for a fresh dose. William Edmonson stopped his cart-horse with a flick of the fingers and looked laconically down at Bushman. He slowly raised a finger and rubbed the side of his beaked nose. 'Well, here she is again, Bushman,' he said.

William's wagon was in good old Yorkshire style. It had been blue, but had faded to a subtle greyish-white with darker bands of colour on the underside of the frame. It was a square-cut wagon with long grooves along the sides, five-foot rear wheels but with a front pair small enough to turn underneath the body for easy moving in cramped farmyards or in narrow winding lanes. The body was a bed of long elm boards sloping down gently towards the back end, easy to shovel out. The elm was smooth, almost shiny with use. The wagon had wooden axles capped by iron boxes to take the wheels.

Bushman looked at the offside back wheel and shook his head. 'I told thee, William, to mind that sill at the station.' William climbed down and they both looked at the wheel. The box had worn itself loose in its socket on the bush, and in places the iron tyre stood clear of the worn felloes. There was nothing else for it, he would have to make a new wheel. Bushman went into the workshop for the jack and his sledge hammer. Being a friend, William was naturally given priority.

Bushman left the wagon up-ended and rolled the heavy wheel into the workshop to look at it more carefully. Then he climbed into the loft and searched among the pile of sawn elm logs until he found a well-seasoned piece of the right size. He brought out into the light a dusty brown length of elm with a hole bored clear through the middle, over fifteen inches long, a foot across, and with its bark trimmed off after it had seasoned for a year with the bark on. Elm was the only timber for a bush, it was tough, it didn't split, it held the ends of the spokes securely. He fixed the log in the vice and began to work it with his adze into the round-ended cylinder which matched the old wheel bush. Once it was shaped, he cut out grooves at either end to take the iron bands which would cramp it together. He worked carefully with the adze, then finished off with the paring knife held in both hands, its long back blade drawn towards him and the shavings falling around his feet on either side. It looked as if it had been turned on a lathe. Now he had to drill holes to take the spoke ends, using a three-foot iron auger from the tool rack and turning it by hand to bite out the spirals of tough wood.

He paused a moment for breath, looked at the finished block, and compared its dimensions, once again, with the worn original, using a pair of solid iron calipers. Next came the spokes, made out of cleft oak. The oak which they stored in the loft came out of the estate woodlands of Gisburn forest, split by foresters in spring when the sap was flowing. Hammered by wedges, the wood broke along its tough fibrous length and was strong enough throughout to take the strain of a wagon load transmitted to the road. The oak clefts were run ragged ended, sometimes split with long shakes where they had seasoned in the loft. Bushman had to shape them into the basic long, smooth strut, with its angled tenon on either end and a pear-shaped cross section. He stood them on the bench and adzed them roughly into shape, planed them down still more and finally, delicately, with a curved wooden spokeshave, trimmed them to their finished perfection. Now, after dinner, would come the job of fixing spokes into the bush. He left them to lie in a regular array on his swept bench and walked back across the yard.

Afternoon sunlight was beginning to penetrate the workshop as he set the bush securely into the waist-high wooden vice and took the first spoke in his hand. With a wooden beetle he tapped it gently into its socket. Then he looked at its angle. He went back and checked the angle of the spokes in the old wheel. No wheel was straight up and down; the sideways traction of a moving horse, the sway of its haunches in the shafts, would soon tear the spokes out of their sockets. It had to be angled to stand the strain, and since the spokes could best carry the wagon's load if they met the ground at right angles, the wheels had also to be angled against the axle so that they leant outwards slightly in relation to the body of the cart. This was a matter of design and strength, and in the same way, in choice of timbers, in shape and construction, each wheel was the perfected result of centuries of experience. Bushman was happy with the angle of his spokes. He took a sledge-hammer, lifted it high above his head and drove each spoke home with a resounding thud. Oak that would last fifty years on the road did not need to be handled gently.

When he loosened the vice, he could lift out a circle of spokes firmly fixed in the central bush. He carried it into the yard and laid it down on the wheel stool. Now he had to make the felloes, the sections of wheel rim, out of pale grey ash which was free from shakes. Rough blocks of ash were maturing in the loft. When they were down and laid on the bench his first job was to plane them flat and smooth and then, using a pattern, mark out the curve for a five-foot wheel. They were adzed and smoothed into shape, mortise holes cut out for the spoke ends, and dowel holes drilled where the half-tenons overlapped. Placed against the star of spokes on the stool, with Bushman and his father heaving on long-handled iron spoke-jacks, mortises and tenons were set in place, and they could tack the felloes lightly together. Now Bushman had a fully assembled wheel, not yet solid, but so designed that when an iron tyre was shrunk on to the felloes, it was bound into one strong unit with a hard rim which would last for a lifetime of use. The blacksmith's shop lay across Thornton Hill, sandwiched tightly into the row of cottages. Bushman had to wait a few days until enough big jobs had accumulated and a full-sized furnace could justifiably be fuelled. The old blacksmith was known for his careful ways. The forge itself, raised above the road, had in front an iron pivot where wheels were held while the red-hot tyres were hammered on to them.

'It's a five footer,' said Bushman. 'Aye,' said the blacksmith, and for a five-foot wheel he brought out over sixteen feet of iron bar, two inches wide, three-quarters of an inch thick. He ran a traveller round the outside of the wheel, and then measured the same distance along the bar, marking it with chalk. Allowing by eye alone for shrinkage, the welding to tie it together, and sufficient contraction to dish the wheel, the blacksmith took his cold chisel and he smashed his hammer down with regular blows, cutting the bar of iron in two. Inside the shop it was forced round by levers into a circle, the flattened ends welded and riveted together. Then, on a great hot bed of glowing coals, played on by hand bellows to keep it even, the heavy tyre was brought to red heat. Four sweating men with long tongs, Bushman among them, carried it outside into the street, laid it on the new wheel and drove it down with hammers around the ash rim. Smoke rose up in clouds, the wheel began to char, and hurriedly buckets of water were thrown time and again on to the glowing metal until it cooled and shrank and bound the wheel tighter together as the wood creaked and the joints were pressed in. The shape became slightly more dished, as Bushman and the blacksmith between them had calculated, and now it matched the old wheel which was being replaced. In an hour or two it was cool enough to be handled.

Bushman was quite accustomed to bowling five-foot wheels down the road as if they were giant hoops, and he cantered along beside this one getting a good run on it so that it would roll under its own weight up beside the house, wobble a little at the corner, but be taken in hand and propelled down the yard. William Edmonson's wagon, backed into a corner against the workshop window, leaned uneasily towards the wall with its axle resting on an iron jack. The new wheel, a square central hole cut into its bush, was wedged into place on the cast iron axle-box, as Bushman split oak wedges from the block and drove them home with a sledge-hammer. He let the jack down and the wagon stood square again, the white ash felloes of the new wheel making an odd contrast beside the chipped and faded blue of its neighbours. Bushman stood back and shook his head sadly. Repainting a wagon was a job he enjoyed, when thrifty farmers would allow it, but such pleasures rarely came to him, save for the few proud folk who commissioned him in advance of May Day. He looked the wheel up and down once again, then turned and walked along the yard and up the narrow pathway for a spell of quiet in the garden.

6

⚜

May Day in Thornton

Nelly had gone to sleep with her fingers crossed and, although they had unaccountably come undone in the night, the magic worked. At six o'clock on the morning of her tenth May Day she could see sunlight streaming across the empty yard. She was downstairs before Bushman and out into the silence. 'Isn't it grand,' she thought, echoing her Mam's turn of phrase, as she gazed up the sunlit village, flooded with golden light. She leant her head against the rough stone of the house corner and breathed in familiar smells, the background of farmyard hay and muck, a quick puff or two of sooty smoke from newly-lit fires and the occasional sweetness blowing from late daffodils in Mr Carr's garden across the road.

Her quiet was disturbed by the rattles and groans of William Edmonson's ancient wagon as it came up from the valley. Nelly pressed herself against the wall when William turned into the yard entrance. He stopped when he saw her. 'Hello, Nelly, up wi' t'lark I see,' and he held out a hand. Nelly grasped the hard palm, felt the easy pull of one strong arm, and sat down beside her friend. It was no longer a hay-wagon, for William had fitted planks across as seats for all the children he would carry that day. They entered the yard in state.

Bushman came out of the door still buttoning his second-best shirt, and reached out his arms to lift Nelly down.

'Morning, William,' he said, 'you're early about.' William smiled sheepishly and confessed, 'Aye, it's about that wheel; the wife wants it painted after all.' So the two of them went into the workshop. Bushman fiddled about in the back and brought out a block of blue paint, put it in the paint grinder and ground out a couple of handfuls of chips into an iron pan. Then he took it across to the house and put it on the fire to melt.

'What's this then?' said Sarah as the smell of bubbling paint filled the kitchen when she came down the stairs. William Edmonson and Bushman were supping tea beside the table. 'It's for Will,' said Bushman and pointed a thumb out at the wagon in the yard. 'It'll never dry in time,' Sarah retorted. The men ignored this obvious remark, for after all, the painting was a woman's notion, put down their cups, and took the melted paint with them to the yard.

Half an hour later William Edmonson poked his smiling face sideways through the back window, 'Nelly,' he said, 'you're all to come with me. Tell your Mam.' 'Oh, thank you, Mr Edmonson,' said Nelly, slightly startled by the sudden appearance. 'But we must have a good song from thee on t'way back,' he added, disappearing before she had time to reply. Nelly told her Mam of William's offer, and so they loaded a basket of sandwiches, cold tea and home-made lemonade into the back of the wagon in the yard.

Mam sent the impatient children to wait beside the love tree with Nelly in charge, to watch the preparations while she got ready herself. As other carts and wagons began to gather, little clouds of dust blew about, lightly powdering the new paint — mostly blue or deep red, with dark lines picked out here and there, the odd yellow cart shining among them, and bright ribbons on horses and whips. The rookery was alert and noisy at all the bustle below. Both the big horse-chestnut tree in its angle between old and new roads and the elms beyond it were full of black spectators, sitting beside their untidy nests and squawking loudly at the display.

Rumbles and rattles could be heard now from every direction. There was the sound of hooves and a smell of horse-sweat. Farmers were dressed to match their teams, and wore billycock hats, waistcoats, and polished boots. Billy-a-Doad rattled down from Bell's Farm behind the Post Office in a maroon wagon fitted with seats and crowded with his children, Kit, Arthur, John, Elsie and Edith, grinning with delight and calling out to their friends. Billy-a-Doad rolled sideways as they turned the corner on to the road and planted his tiny feet firmly on the boards to steady himself. Then he gave a comfortable smile as the horses drew to a halt beside the Post Office wall.

Bushman and his father were standing together on the Post Office steps to watch the slowly forming procession. The post round had started and finished early that day, for Wright-Jack had been down at the station with his trolley to meet the seven o'clock train and deliver the first letters as he made his way into the village. They both smiled and nodded as the maroon wagon and its load of children came round the corner. 'My, Billy-a-Doad's in good time,' said Bushman. 'Yes,' said Wright-Jack, 'I spoke to him this morning when I took the post. He was up early. His wife can't get this baby started at all.' 'What did you tell him, father?' 'I told him he should assist Providence, get her into t'gig and take her up by t'mount yonder, then down that steep hill into Earby. "She'll start then," I said. But I see she's not coming today.' The sudden vision of a perplexed, owlish Billy-a-Doad caught half-way to Earby as an impromptu midwife amused them both. Billy chose this moment to wave; Bushman put his hands on his hips, threw back his head, and roared with laughter, while Wright-Jack raised his cane in acknowledgment.

William Edmonson re-appeared from his farm down the Old Road, a spray of cowslips pinned to his jacket, his wife, in white dress and flowery hat, on his arm. They crossed the main road to the love tree and William, full of good humour, made an exaggerated flourish and bowed to Nelly. She stood in white on the stone seat, her face crinkled in the struggle between solemnity and a smile, but managed a rather unsteady curtsey before the first giggle escaped. 'Well, miss,' said William, 'I'll bring the carriage round for you,' and he went into the yard for the blue wagon.

Carriages were actually beginning to appear, for the gentry generally arrived after the farmers. Nelly watched the commotion at the house of Mr Carr, the solicitor, which stood sideways to the road across from the Post Office. The odd gothic back door opened, and Anna, Carr's tall, surprised-looking maid, peered out in frightened expectation of seeing the dark figure of John James Brown, quarryman and village madman in a small way, who for the past month had been paying her his lecherous springtime attentions. He was not mad enough to be locked away, but his wild appearance, mutterings and gestures, were sufficient to frighten any child who met him. Nelly always crossed the road to avoid him. Anna had found him outside the back door one evening, gazing at her hungrily, and had rushed inside to slam the oak behind her. She said she could feel his eyes through two inches of timber. He had appeared, waiting, on the grass outside every evening for a month. She was clearly relieved today to see no dark figure with staring eyes.

Anna ran to open the front door as the coachman brought the carriage smartly round. Nelly and the children watched Mrs Carr, in elegant brown, and her three grown-up daughters, in a matching set of pastel dresses, being handed into their seats. Then Mr Carr himself appeared, dapper and kindly, with a little moustache and an absent-minded smile. As he put one foot on the carriage step his wife leaned across. 'Arthur, where's the lunch?' He paused in thought, then smiled. 'Well, it's all rather sub judice my dear, since you and cook couldn't agree on the cold meat, but I'll see to it.' He scurried back inside.

Now the pattern was broken. Hearty singing echoed up

from the rock horse stables where the quarry animals were kept, and soon a heavy cart emerged, drawn by the two rock horses, no longer dusty but groomed and shiny, their harness half hidden by yellow ribbons. Quarrymen surrounded the wagon. Mr Nightingale rode behind on his own horse, his hair as sleek and glossy as his mount's coat. Barrel Bradley, one beefy hand on the harness, proudly led the cart into position just behind Billy-a-Doad. To everyone's amazement, for how it had been contrived nobody knew, John James Brown's old mother, the only person who could control him, sat in the back. She was not quite as dirty as usual, in an incredible brownish green dress blackened with wear, and clasping an old umbrella to match. Her little eyes looked fiercely around her, and John James himself walked submissively by her side of the cart, kicking up the dust with his clogs.

Other folk on foot began to crowd around the love tree. Mill workers, farmers' labourers, servants, they were all prepared for an outing, in their best clothes, thick and heavy, cut to last through the years rather than for mere comfort on a hot spring day. Then Mr Morris, the rector, came trotting down the hillside, a plump cob beneath his plump thighs. He had put on a top-hat in honour of the occasion and raised it cheerily to everyone. 'Well, well; a fine turn-out,' he shouted generally, and began to marshal the line, closing gaps, waving imperiously at Barrel when the quarry cart backed suddenly into the road.

William Edmonson brought his wagon round and into line. Mam sat at the back beside the food and the children scrambled up the back wheels to join her. Bushman, under instructions, brought out a pair of steps and helped his mother on to the seat beside William Edmonson. 'That'll do,' she remarked, arranging her basket and waving at Bushman to take away the steps, while settling down with complacency to wait.

At last the sound of quiet horses could be heard coming

at a steady pace up Thornton Drag. Mrs Smith, the land-owner, the village proprietor, would soon be here. She was driven in her victoria past the waiting line of wagons, carts and carriages. She wore a grey silk dress, one small bunch of flowers pinned to her hat, and nodded her fine head coolly to everyone as she passed; but the little Skye terrier beside her began to leap up and down and yap furiously at every dog in the village. 'Be quiet, Mackintosh,' said Mrs Smith and tapped its nose. The dog settled down, looking bottled indignation, on the seat beside her. Mr Morris raised his hat as the victoria glided past him and Mrs Smith smiled a little, her pale-blue eyes surveying his red face.

The coachman had his instructions, for he took Mrs Smith and Mackintosh away up the village and through the gates of the manor house. The procession of vehicles and the crowd of watchers by the love tree waited once again. Then the victoria emerged with new passengers, Mr Sutcliffe, retired mill-owner, and his unmarried, pale daughter of thirty, wearing an improbable lilac dress.

Now the procession could start. Mr Morris had been waiting impatiently, urging his horse up and down the line. He raised his arm as a signal. But before he could lower it again a sudden commotion distracted everyone. Amid great cursings and swearings they could hear the sound of a cart-wheel grating against a gate post. Hartley Procter was late. Living at Chester Farm, half-way up the village and close to the start of the procession he had not bothered to hurry. Now, with the customary dandelion in his buttonhole, black hair sticking out in greasy spikes and dust all down the side of his black suit, he was heaving and shoving at the cartwheel, its bush jammed tight against the wooden post. 'Bloody hell,' he said, 'get over, damn you.' Bushman ran up to help and between them they got the cart round. Hartley Procter scrambled into his seat without giving any thanks, looked furiously at his wife, lashed the horses, and rattled off to push his way into the line.

Now the horses moved at a steady walk up the hill past the manor house and rectory gate, down the far side with drags on the wheels, leaving Thornton hidden in its fold of ground. They came to the church among its gravestones and beech trees, bore right around it and took the tree-lined road to Nutter Cote field, a little patch of level ground which lay in the valley where road and canal almost met. There they found the Earby Prize Brass Band with cornets, trumpets, tubas, and french horns polished so brightly that they looked too hot to hold in the sunshine. All the children rushed over to listen. Their mothers and fathers chose good picnic spots, and when the band finished the children slowly drifted back. Family groups were dotted around the field, mothers sitting upright and unpacking the food, fathers lying on their sides, heads supported on one arm. The gentry had drawn up their carriages to form a defensive half circle, looking out over the field, and were picnicking in state. When the talking died down you could hear the unharnessed horses tearing up grass at the side of the hedge.

The rasping note of a hunting horn brought all the children running over to Mr Morris. As his cheeks subsided and he lowered the short silver tube, a little whispered chorus of 'Well, well; well, well,' came from the bigger lads. He smiled benignly. 'Well, well, children, so you're all ready for the races. Well, indeed. Will you all make a line against the hedge there, and we can get ready.' Chattering children rushed or wandered over to the hedge side as Mr Morris, like a latter-day pied-piper, raised his horn to summon the parents. But they were already on their way, with half the arrangements secretly made beforehand.

Mr Morris formally announced the Mayday cricket match, ladies to bat first, men to use bat handles only and to bowl underarm. He declared that Mrs Smith had consented to be nonplaying ladies' captain, with Mrs Hartley as her assistant. Mrs Hartley, in a billowing light-grey dress, puffed out a smile. Bushman, lazily throwing and catching a ball with one hand on his hip, now in his prime as a cricketer, was the obvious choice as men's captain. When his name was announced, he threw the ball lightly to Mrs Hartley, who caught it against her ample bosom and glared defiance. It was to be a case of strong personality against skill in the game.

Once the children's sports were over the umpires, Mr Morris and Mr Carr, set out with a gaggle of children at their heels to put up stumps. Bushman and his friends, crowding round a barrel of ale on the back of a cart, were waved on to the field and spread themselves off-handedly about, keen to demonstrate that this irregular game needed no careful, scientific placing of slips and deep fielders. Mrs Hartley marshalled her team of energetic young girls and formidable married ladies, then marched out to bat first.

Bushman, champion bowler of Thornton, capered around the far wicket. Bowling underarm was a poor weak substitute for the thundering run which struck terror in the hearts of village batsmen. He drew back his arm and flicked the ball to Mrs Hartley who stubbornly put her bat in the way, carefully placing it down like a posser into a dollytub of wet clothes. The ball struck the bat with a dull thud and lay there. Mrs Hartley looked at it, then helpfully bent down and threw it back, as if she were playing a game with the children. Bushman sighed and ran his hands through his hair. In his enthusiasm to use up energy he wasted a considerable number of overs hurling bouncers which more often than not lost themselves in the ladies' wide and heavy skirts. The umpires refused his persistent appeals for 'leg-before-wicket'. Mr Carr politely pointed out that he couldn't see the ladies' legs. Bushman was getting nowhere, and the ladies' score grew in dribs and drabs of little sneaky runs and occasional wides when the ball hit a grass tussock and shot off sideways. The rector signalled these with gusto to Wright-Jack, scoring diligently beside the wheels of Mrs Smith's victoria.

In desperation Bushman called over John James Brown from deep behind the wicket. 'Here, see if tha can bowl,' he said casually, tossing the ball over. Perhaps sheer brute strength would succeed where skill had failed. John James' bouncers were frightening to watch, as he worked up his face, curled his lips in a snarl, and windmilled his arms, both of them, before releasing the ball wildly from one or the other. His first ball nearly brained Barrel Bradley, who was crouched double close to the wicket at silly mid-on, waiting for a catch. The second bounded wildly past Mrs Robinson, the other batswoman, as she cowered before the wicket. Even Billy-a-Doad, a lightning little wicket-keeper, couldn't reach it. Mrs Hartley bellowed at her partner to run, and thundered into the crease. The next ball went true; sailing from John James' grimy hand it struck Mrs Hartley firmly on the corsets with a dull thud and fell to the ground. No man had the courage to shout 'Leg before'. Mrs Hartley made no sound, but clutched her stomach and glared furiously down the pitch.

The rector called Mr Carr over, and they conferred seriously. Bushman hurried across, to be told that John James must be taken off. 'Ah'm not bloody going . . .' he grumbled, but at last shambled off the field, torn waistcoat flapping, to throw himself down to sulk in the grass beside Wright-Jack. There he amused himself by chewing grass, spitting, muttering occasional curses and staring Miss Sutcliffe out of countenance as she sat beside Mrs Smith in the victoria. She became quite disturbed by this pale, freckled, flabby face with its deep, staring eyes. Sometimes he propped his head against a wheel and looked at her normally, but at other times he lay flat on his back and stared upside down. If anything she found that more upsetting.

Meanwhile Bushman returned to his unrewarding job as bowler. The ladies' score had mounted towards fifty runs when at last he discovered the technique. If he trundled the ball fast along the ground there was every probability that the lady batsmen would swing wildly over the top of it, that it would pass under their skirts and, if not deflected by the roughness of the ground, it might hit the wicket. It worked well, while Billy-a-Doad leapt nimbly about and solved the problem from his end. Every time a lady stepped forward to meet a grubber Billy was there, his hand scooping the ball up beside her skirts, his booted foot kicking the stumps to make the bails fall. Then, in his light voice, face gaily turned towards Mr Carr, eyes glinting, he would call 'How's that?' Mr Carr found the claims hard to resist. Soon the ladies had only one wicket left.

Mrs Hartley's team had failed her. She found that her eleventh batswoman had disappeared. No one else would take on the responsibility. Nelly's Mam refused point blank, saying that she was stiff and her bad leg hurt. So, to Bushman's amazement, the last batswoman marched out like a ship in full sail, her dress billowing, and took her stance at the crease, bold as brass. 'It's Bertha Hartley again! She can't do that!' Bushman turned in protest to the rector. The umpires consulted, heads close together, and ended with a chuckle. 'I can see no difficulty,' was the reply, and Mr Carr added sagely, 'Yes, perfectly acceptable procedure.'

Mrs Hartley remained at the wicket, and her technique also had improved. She blocked carefully and well, keeping the bat down, one boot always firmly in the crease. The ladies' score rose slowly and stood at seventy-eight runs as Mrs Hartley used all her cunning to remain facing the bowler. Barrel Bradley had crept even closer to the bat as this dull blocking game continued and at last his courage was rewarded. The ball rose a few, bare inches from the ground, to bounce from the tip of Mrs Hartley's bat. Barrel dived desperately. His fingertips just caught the ball as he fell with an earth-shaking thud. But he flicked it in the air again, to catch it firmly, one handed, as he thrashed over on to his back, legs flailing. 'Out,' said the rector firmly, and Mrs

Hartley marched off the field to cheers and claps from all the spectators.

The men came into bat against heavy odds, holding the bat awkwardly by its thick end, totally surrounded by a horde of young fielders. The children came out to help their mothers and stood in the long grass of the outfield chewing stalks, turning cartwheels, and shrieking with delight if the ball came their way. The men's team was almost humiliated. Bushman refused to be inhibited by the odd end of the bat and attempted to slog as he always did. One or two wild shots went off at amazing angles from the round handle, and there were some thunderous runs made to loud shriekings from the children as the ball made its erratic progress towards the wicket-keeper. But Bushman was bowled out by a ball which trickled uncertainly from bump to bump, appeared to swerve round his powerful stroke, and rested against the offside stump, dislodging the bail. The men's team vanished at an alarming rate. Hartley Procter limped in, made a few sarcastic pokes at the ball, and limped out again. Billy-a-Doad's elegant swing and swift movements were useless on such a field and against such opponents. Soon they had only two batsmen left, and almost thirty runs to make.

Barrel Bradley came in. After watching solemnly from the edge of the field he reckoned he had the measure of the women's tactics. He set himself to block, carefully placing the bat handle down in the precise track of the ball and leaving it to lie in the middle of the pitch. Then he would sneak a run while the ladies and children fought to pick up the ball and erratically hurled it somewhere within range of the wicket. Mrs Hartley, always at the post of danger and responsibility, had undertaken to keep wicket. She hurled her bulk from side to side, large pads, fastened only at the ankle, flapping loosely about her skirts. Somehow she stopped most of the wildly thrown balls with one part or another of her body, but often Barrel got two runs when the ball flew wide over her head. Nettle joined in the game, adding to the confusion by seizing the ball and carrying it off in her teeth. She growled at the children who tried to take it and, while Nelly was summoned hurriedly from the long grass, the men got another five runs.

The men's score mounted to sixty-nine, only nine runs behind the women's total, while Barrel continued with his logical game. Steady little John Riley backed him up at the other end. Barrel was in good humour now, pleased with himself, and he had taken to playfully standing to attention in front of the crease, holding the bat end with one beefy hand, and lowering its handle just as the ball reached him. One ball rolled at right angles from the bat to stop against his toe-cap. 'How's that!' yelled all the children. The rector replied 'Not out! But if you're too clever again, Barrel, it'll be out next time.'

The game continued, the men by now only two runs behind. Young Eileen Wilkinson had been given a chance to bowl and hurled a bouncer in the general direction of Barrel Bradley. It was clearly going to be wide and Barrel ignored it. Mrs Hartley turned and reached out one leg, stopping the ball with her pads, but at the same moment her other foot clicked loudly against the stumps and the bails fell off. 'How's that?' screamed the children again. The rector and Mr Carr nodded to each other; the rector took out his watch. 'Out,' he said ruthlessly. 'What do you mean, "Out"?' yelled Barrel Bradley 'Out' said the two umpires again, looking at each other for support. Barrel Bradley threw down his bat in disgust and stumped off the pitch.

The last batsman, young Kit Wilkinson, came on and was bowled out after an over and a half by the first ball which was actually in line with the wicket. The ladies had won. All the children cheered. Mrs Hartley staggered off the field and collapsed impressively beside a can of cold tea, hurling her pads into the hedge.

Everyone was thirsty, and the day was still hot and clear. Mothers no longer sat upright in their places, but walked over to see friends and stretched out their legs a little on the crushed grass. Then the band set off across the field on the way back to Earby. They moved out of the gate, still playing and along the road. The sound died away a little as the trees closed in behind them and finally they broke step to climb over the stile and take the little hillside path to town. Farmers wandered slowly over to their horses and led them back between the shafts, buckling on the harness with practised fingers. Tired children were lifted in bundles into the wagons for a ride back to Thornton. Mothers collected cups and bags to put in their empty baskets. William Edmonson beckoned over the hedge as the Rileys pulled their stiff-legged mother to the gate. If he had a cartload full of children he was as happy as could be. Bushman was left with the cricketers. He would find his own way back. The family travelled in slow and stately fashion and watched a sunlit world pass by.

When the weary army reached the top of Thornton they looked down beyond the rectory wall to the sloping village green opposite the school. The boys had laid out long desks and trestle tables ready for the feast. Mothers and daughters bustled back into their houses and came out again with home-made cakes, meat rolls and boiled hams, cups and plate and old sheets for table-cloths. The tables were spread and set down in ranks on the sloping grass. Village worthies, old people and children were seated and the food laid out. Then the fire under Mrs Lambert's copper set-pan roared high, and pairs of girls staggered to and from her wash-house, carrying heavy tea-urns to the table.

Nelly's grandfather, being an office-holder, had his place at the head of a table, magnificent in his full suit, watch-chain and curly-brimmed hat. There were no shirt-sleeves for Wright-Jack. He took a comb out of his waistcoat pocket and slowly combed his silky white beard. Then he stopped, his comb still half out, his eyes wide open in amazement.

In the sudden silence everyone heard Miss Sutcliffe's

suppressed scream. She rounded the foot of Wright-Jack's table, hand to her mouth, holding her skirt, running as fast as a plain spinster of thirty could be expected to run. 'What in the Lord's name . . .!' grunted Wright-Jack as he shot to his feet. John James Brown was roaring round the table after Miss Sutcliffe. He clutched half a two-pound loaf in his hand; but his deep eyes were intent on the lilac dress. A boiled ham, a pile of sandwiches and several cups and saucers bounced over the grass as he caught the end of a table.

John James, red-hot as a boiler from sun and beer, began to yell thick words while he ran. The rector shouted 'Stop the fool,' and blew a loud blast on his horn. Miss Sutcliffe staggered on up the green towards home and safety, one arm flailing for balance, the other still clutching her dress. John James came close behind her, roaring like a bull, his waistcoat and baggy trousers flapping. Miss Sutcliffe turned her head, white-faced and desperate. The whole village stood beside the half-eaten feast, silent in amazement, watching the race draw away from them as John James closed on his prey.

Then a group of stragglers from the cricket field appeared at the top of Thornton hill. A chorus of yells from the tables alerted Barrel and his brother, Bill Bradley. They moved quickly, for John James was now breathing heavily only a yard behind Miss Sutcliffe. The Bradleys ran across, and with surprising speed Barrel stuck out a foot. John James fell heavily. He grunted and gasped, releasing the half-loaf, which lodged in the gutter. Then he yelled aloud and began to struggle upwards. Bill promptly sat on his head, and Barrel on his legs. They remained on guard, each with a mug of tea and a sandwich, ignoring his curses and occasional convulsions. At last John James' mother appeared to lead him away, beating his head with her umbrella as she went. Miss Sutcliffe disappeared inside the manor gates, her virtue safe, not to re-appear in public for days. Talk began and then a little ripple of smiles and chuckles. The rector hastily stood up to present the prizes, and giggling children were pushed forward one by one.

The last crumbs, plates, and cups full of tea-leaves were cleared away. Boys and men carried long desks back inside the school and arranged them around the walls, leaving the scrubbed floor clear and open. Groups of people chatted and drifted home. The lingering children were called inside, for although it was still light and sunny they were sleepy and excited. Mothers and fathers had the evening on their minds. Then a light-hearted Bushman said 'Let's take the lasses to t'dance with us tonight, mother.' 'Nay,' said Mam; but Nelly and Annie begged 'Mam, please can we come?' and Mam gave way. She could not resist both her sportsman husband and her own two girls. So they washed their faces in cold water and went upstairs to put on their fine white long dresses with the little capes above. They left their clogs under the bed and took down Sunday shoes from the rack on the kitchen wall. Sarah wore white lace at her neck instead of black, and a large cameo brooch. Bushman had his best suit with the braided lapels. They felt fine and grand, strolling up the middle of the road as evening began to fall.

Once inside the building, the school had no feeling of day-time lessons at all. Little groups of neighbours were transformed by their best clothes. The fiddler from Gubshill was tuning and soon he began to play. Mam and Dad joined in the dance, up and down, hands together, in and out. When the fiddler broke a string, everyone stopped and chatted till he was ready again. Nelly and Annie sat demurely in a corner and watched the excitement. A waltz began. There was Billy-a-Doad dancing like a goblin, red-cheeked, his pointed feet darting about as if he didn't own them. His plain solid wife was away, of course, but then she had been chosen for work and not for show. She ran his farm and bore him eight children, but she was not his match at a waltz, and when Billy-a-Doad took a delighted Nelly through her paces, she felt as if she were flying.

It was getting late, and as the dusk fell they lit candles on the window-sills. When the door next opened the firm figure of their grandmother stood at the edge of the candlelight. She beckoned to the girls and they moved out into the darkness of the village. Hugging Grandma's arms they crunched down the gravel to the cottage door. They heaved themselves upstairs and stood a flickering candle on the dresser. They were almost too tired to undress. Nelly and Annie snuggled down into the soft lumpy mattress, pulled the covers around their necks, and fell asleep without a whisper.

7

Ghosts and a Goose

May Day, school, summer days of paddling in the beck, running errands and helping with the hay passed by, and suddenly the children found themselves deep in winter again. Time roared along, and the series of fireside stories brought them ever nearer to Christmas.

Fire shone in the children's faces. Dad stretched back in his armchair. Mam sat straight-backed on the settee with the cat beside her. In a moment's silence they could hear the wind howling in the trees outside. The boys whispered to each other and turned round from the fire. 'Tell us a tale, Dad.' Dad looked at them solemnly and winked. In a dreadful voice he said, 'Shall I give thee a tale to chill thy bones?' They looked back at him with solemn eyes. 'Oh, aye, Dad,' so Bushman got up and walked over to the little cupboard beside the door. He rummaged in the back and brought out an old worn book, the back broken and title page long since torn away. As he sat down again and opened it he looked at the children as if in warning. 'Have you heard tell of the Hand of Glory?' he said. The boys silently shook their heads. Nelly moved the lamp up to his elbow so that he could see clearly, and he began to read, deepening his voice to suit the words.

'Once, many years ago in the days of our ancestors, there stood a small obscure farmhouse hidden far in the remote fells of Yorkshire. It was an old, old house which seemed to have risen out of the ground rather than been built by men, for its low walls were made of great uneven stones, and bracken covered its roof, held down against the wind by yet more slabs of grey limestone. It was long and rough, half given over to beasts and half for men, like a rocky outcrop of the ground, protected against the fierce wind and rains of that remote hillside by a few broken thorn trees.

'There, bent old farmer Braithwaite and his older wife scratched out a living. After years of hardship and isolation they were silent, slow-moving folk, but ready indeed to welcome any passing acquaintance, and hospitable when they left their cows and came to sit before the fire of an evening. Their only help in both house and farm was supplied by the strong arms of young Sarah, an orphan girl, who lived with them like a daughter. They were far from other folk, out of sight of the village. Each Sunday a laborious hour passed by on the walk to church along rutted lanes and muddy paths, and another hour was spent in their return.'

Dad looked up for a moment at the intent faces of his children in the firelight, smiled to himself in satisfaction, and continued his tale.

'Strange things had been heard and spoken of in the village that winter as the wind howled across the wastes. Fear dwelt in people's minds, and old stories of wild beasts, unearthly legends of the barghests with their frenzied staring eyes and older memories, which told of withered figures, horrible to the sight, threatening loathsome death to their beholders, were heard at the fireside. Shepherds had found the body of an old man dressed in rags, high up on the screes. Some folk said he had died of a dreadful contagion. They had brought him down in haste and buried his skeleton form with little ceremony in the newly enclosed graveyard. The first soul to be buried there and eternally in peril, never certain to sleep in peace. Again, distant sounds like the baying of dogs were heard high up on rocky slopes among the sink-holes and hidden valleys. Men turned ever more to the old charms

76

of their past and sent their little children out on to the wild slopes to bring home branches of mountain ash full of glossy red berries. These they nailed above their house doors, as a solemn warning to unwanted visitors.

'It was now deep into winter and for days the bitter wind had blown fiercely across the fell-sides, to howl around the sunken roof of Braithwaite's farm. Early one cold morning, as she huddled in her cloak towards the shippon, young Sarah found the branches of mountain ash blown from their place above the door, and scattered, as if by some malicious hand, into the far corners of the yard. She brought one battered sprig, still clad in withered berries, into the house and laid it on the wooden settle beside the black heavy Bible. Almost, it seemed, the girl invoked God's aid in the dreadful visitation that was to come.

'That wild night a high moon shone coldly and fitfully from behind thin clouds which chased across its face, casting a dismal gleam on the farm, the white walls of sheep pens and the little wisps of smoke appearing from the squat chimney stack. The strong wind bent even those hardy thorn trees which had survived long winters on the bitter hillside. It lifted the thatch around the eaves, seeking to penetrate every cranny and threaten the warmth within. Supper-time grew near and the farm dogs were more restless than usual. They prowled to and fro, sniffing at the foot of the door, but when Sarah opened it they refused to be driven outside. With hair bristling, cars down, and legs pressed against the floor, they whined and backed away. Suddenly there was a knock, although no one had heard steps approaching. Old Braithwaite raised his head, Sarah put down the kettle, they looked at each other and listened. A deep silence prevailed throughout the house. The dogs ceased to whimper and cowered back towards the fire. Then a continuous knocking began. Braithwaite moved reluctantly to the door, unbarred and opened it.

'A hooded figure could be seen, dimly lit by the cloudy

moon, standing motionless before the door. In size it might have been an old woman shrunken with age, hardly capable of tottering from the fireside to the churchyard. The figure stepped over the threshold, and in a harsh, cracked voice asked for a bite to eat and a bed for the night. All three felt a chill fear deep in their hearts at this dismal apparition, its black hood pulled down to hide its unknown face from the firelight. They seemed to have no power to protest, and as if in a trance Sarah brought a wooden platter with bread and cheese, whilst Mrs Braithwaite slowly poured a mug of ale. The hooded creature took Braithwaite's chair before the fire, chewed a little food, made as if to drink from the mug, and left the remnants standing on the table without a word of thanks.

'The evening drew on, the fire burned low, the silence deepened. No one felt inclined to speak, and the ever-increasing shriek of the wind invaded their minds. At length Braithwaite pulled himself to his feet and, in a weak, uncertain voice, offered the unwelcome visitor a bed of straw above the cattle. The strange figure remained immovable, the great hood sunk down upon its breast. Then it raised one shrivelled hand, pointed sharply at the fire and its chair, making clear that no persuasion would raise it from its seat, and resumed its accustomed posture. Braithwaite and his wife hesitated on the edge of the firelight, then climbed up the steep stairs to their bedroom above. Sarah's sleeping place was on the oaken settle, her head resting on a cushion and her cloak around her. That ominous night, as unknown fears coursed through her body, she experienced an overwhelming force of sleep pressing down her eyelids. Yet she knew that all was not well, and as her head sank reluctantly on the hard cushion and her eyes closed, she struggled to raise the lids and still observe the dark and menacing figure beside her.

'For a while the figure sat still, hardly seeming to breathe, as if a living corpse without heart in its body, and no light could show its face. Then slowly it rose from the chair, and as it rose its shape began to change. The figure grew tall and broad, though still in the same black cloak which seemed to fit itself to this immense apparition by some ghostly magic. It turned its head slowly round the room until its gaze rested on Sarah. Now she sensed a red gleam of watchful eyes in the shadows below the hood. It stood still for a moment longer then reached inside its cloak and pulled out a small object, holding it towards the invisible face, almost as if it were kissing the thing, whatever it might be. As the firelight flickered for a second Sarah saw it clearly. It could only be one thing. It was a withered brown hand, a dead hand, cut off at the wrist, blackened as if by fire, but complete with long curved fingernails, shrivelled skin and tendons. She could neither close nor open her eyes and only with tremendous effort was she able to keep her breathing steady. Her hands gripped the little stem of mountain ash tightly, crushing the bunch of berries against her palm.

'Again the dark figure reached inside its cloak and this time brought forth a short yellow candle. Now it was intent on its unearthly business. It placed the candle on the palm and, reaching out with the tongs, took a burning branch and held it to the wick until the candle caught light. Then, holding the hand before it, the figure paced around the room muttering incantations in a deep and menacing voice. Sarah's eyes began to close despite every effort of her will. Almost overpowering desire for sleep came over her. She could hear the deep voice pouring out strange syllables in her ear. Sounds beyond her understanding save for the muttered invocation, 'O Hand of Glory', which concluded every sonorous period. For a moment her eyes closed completely and it was only with a terrible effort that she forced them a little way apart. The figure turned towards her, and again she saw a red flash of eyes in the blackness. Her body felt heavy and her breathing was slow and regular. The figure seemed satisfied and turned away.

'It glided over to the window, unbarred the rough shutters and pulled them back to reveal the wild sky and black hills lit by a dismal moon. Then it laid the hand, glowing and dreadful in the light of the candle, on the stone sill. It stood behind the candle as its black hooded shadow filled the room, swallowing Sarah and her settle in its immensity. More deep words came out, urgent now and commanding. The candle flame flared up high, tall and blue, as if it were a beacon shining out into the night. The figure moved over to the doorway, lifted the bar, opened it and stood on the threshold. Sarah lay on her settle, eyes half-open, unable to move. She could see beyond the grim figure the wild slopes of the fells, half lit by the cold moon. Across them lights were moving, pale and flickering in the distance, and as they came near she could see, across the far side of the beck, shapes like great grey dogs with glowing saucer eyes and hear their wild howlings.

'Somehow, how she never knew, she reached out and seized the black Bible. Then, painfully and slowly, she dragged herself to her feet and with incredible care, hardly breathing for fear of attracting the dark figure on the threshold, she moved across to the stairs. The giant dogs were nearer now and behind them appeared other misty shapeless figures, rising from deep holes in the ground. For a moment a deep and awful silence prevailed as, writhing like solid mists, they moved towards the house. The dark hooded figure stepped out to meet them.

'Sarah crawled up the stairs, forcing her body with every step, and came to old Braithwaite's bedside. She seized his arm as it lay on the cover and shook him with all the strength that she had left. He did not move, he lay there as if he were dead, with just a faint breath of air coming from his nostrils. He was chained fast in sleep by the Hand of Glory. Sarah collapsed in despair for a moment and then wildly pulled herself round on her knees to the other side of the bed. She had little strength left as she vainly tried to wake his wife, who also appeared to be in the sleep of Death. Now that she knelt beside the window Sarah could see in the cold cadaverous moonlight a host of weird creatures, swathed in funereal gowns, dancing around the black stranger. Their appearance was terrible to behold and Sarah tried to hide her eyes, but time and again she was drawn back to look at that awful scene. The black figure rose up like a ghastly totem within their circle and ever and again he would turn to point a menacing finger towards the house where she crouched in terror. Now he began to lead them to the door.

'As the howling grew louder an unearthly blue light shone and began to flood like a loathsome fluid up the stairs from below. The whole house seemed to change. Black stains of mould appeared on the walls. Rotten fungus ate away at the thatch above her head, and the slimy floorboards began to sag under the weight of their own rottenness. Slowly she turned towards the bed and looked at old Braithwaite. The flesh appeared to be melting from his face. Deep, haggard eye-sockets revealed nothing but blackness, and bony gums appeared beneath his wrinkled lips. Like a mouldering corpse he lay, infested with the lurid light of decay. Then, horror of horrors, as she looked down at her own hand lying on the cover, she saw the flesh begin to thin and the bones of her own skeleton appearing through the wasted skin. With her hands to her face she tottered to the stairs.

'Now she shuffled like a moving corpse, hardly knowing why she still persevered and forcing herself against the strange painful pressure of the dreadful light which flowed up the stairs. The black figure and its weird followers were almost at the door. The candle on the Hand of Glory blazed up ever more fiercely to greet them. Sarah slowly turned, her skeleton face drawn towards the light, and driven by some deep impulse she moved towards it until she stood beside the table. Her eye fell on the untouched mug of ale. Suddenly, in desperation, without any clear thought of what she was doing, she grasped the mug and with agonizing slowness hurled it at the candle. There was a hiss, a smell of steam, and all became dark in the house. It was as if the whole world had ceased to exist. The wind was silent. No sound came from outside the door. But in the dim light of the dying fire Sarah could see her hands, and they were young again. She turned towards the door and found that her legs could move freely. With desperate energy Sarah rushed across the room, slammed the door to, and barred it right in the face of the black figure. Then she collapsed, exhausted, beside the fire. There was a noise upstairs, a creaking of floorboards, and Braithwaite and his wife came rushing down, rubbing the sleep from their eyes and asking what was the matter.

'Before Sarah could answer heavy thuds began against the door. The panels groaned and moved under the weight. Still the noise continued, increasing in speed and intensity, beating to the impulse of a racing heart. They looked at each other, and Braithwaite took down his blunderbuss from the wall. Would it have any effect against their inhuman enemy? Sarah and his wife between them shoved over the wooden settle and jammed it against the door. But the beating continued louder and louder, the settle jarred and moved as splinters of wood appeared around the door-frame. Nothing but terror could come from outside that night, and now the creatures were dancing round the house. They could hear the shrieks and howlings from all sides and sense the deadly dangers which threatened them wherever they turned.

'Sarah, driven by some inexplicable impulse, looked again at the withered hand, lying in a small pool of ale. She approached it slowly, hesitantly. It did not move, the stub of candle still stuck to its yellow palm. She reached out a finger towards it, then, with an effort, turned away. It was as if some outside force drew her against her will to the Hand of Glory. For a moment the noise at the door ceased. Sarah's young ears caught a faint noise by the window. What could it be? She peered across the room to see. The hand was moving! It was alive, crawling horribly, painfully, on its broken knuckles, until the ridged fingers scratched frantically at the window. It reared up against the glass like a great insect, making despairing efforts to escape. Then it fell back and twitched on the still.

'They all shuddered, drawing closer together. A sharp rap on the window froze their blood. Sarah raised her eyes and saw the hooded figure, black against the moonlit sky, beckoning her with one ghostly hand. Despite her fear she found herself on her feet and moving forward. As she approached the window the figure pointed commandingly to the hand, which now lay still as if in obedience. Sarah felt a terrible compulsion. Her own hand moved towards the withered horror. She could not restrain herself. Then she felt its clammy wrinkled skin against her own warm palm. As her heart bounded in terror the shrivelled fingers took hold of her wrist and she felt the bones press hard into her flesh. Now she had no choice, human impulse and the silent commands of the black figure all worked together. Trembling, she unlatched the one small, hinged pane, reached frantically through the opening and shook the hand loose into the night air.

'All noises ceased instantly. Nothing could be heard but the wind howling in the trees as Sarah collapsed on to the table, burying her head in her hands. Braithwaite and his wife, still shaking with fear, rushed to her aid, soothed and comforted her. All night they sat beside the fire, their hands on blunderbuss and axes. All night they waited, trembling at every sound, stoking up the fire in silence as the moon travelled across the sky, slowly, hour by hour. At last cold dawn appeared and Braithwaite peered cautiously out from all sides, but they waited for full sun before they unbarred the door. There were no signs at all, no footprints in the muddy yard, no bruises and scars on the door despite the terrible beating it had been given. Nothing except the yellow stub of a candle, lying half-buried in the mud outside the window.'

83

Dad closed the old book. The family sat without moving, staring into the fire. As he had got deeper into the story the children had moved closer and closer to Mam. Now the wind outside sounded near and threatening; it whistled in the chimney and raised flames in the fire, moving black shadows in far corners of the room. Dad chuckled, winked again at the boys and got up from his chair. He walked over to the front door and took down his coat.

'Nay, Will,' said Mam, 'tha's not going out tonight.' 'Aye, lass,' said Bushman, it wasn't often he called Mam 'lass'. 'It's the grand raffle at t'Pickhill. Tha's not afraid to be left at home?' 'Don't be daft,' said Mam sharply and disapprovingly. 'You'd best be off.' Dad said 'Good night' and opened the door, letting in a howl of wind. After two steps the sound of his boots disappeared. The village pub had been closed when he was a boy and now he faced a two-mile walk in either direction simply to get a drink. Nelly and Annie, little girls still at eleven and nine, shuddered and looked at each other. How could Dad set off down the dark road to Elslack under the swaying black trees on such a night and after such a tale? They crept upstairs, whispering comfortingly, and got into bed. Next door the boys were wrapping their shirt-tails about their legs and being howling ghosts all over the room. Nelly shivered deliciously, thankful for having a warm house, a sister beside her, and neighbours in the village close by.

She heard Mam come upstairs, saw a flicker of candle-light from under the door, and heard the big bed creak as she got in and turned over. The house was quiet. She must have fallen asleep. Suddenly, there was a bang at the front door and footsteps below. Nelly and Annie shot up in bed and grabbed each other's hands. They sat still in the darkness, their hearts beating. Then they recognized the heavy tread on the stairs. It was only Dad, back from the Pickhill. He climbed slowly up in the dark and they heard him strike a match to light the candle next door.

Everything was all right and the girls began to settle down to sleep again. But then they heard a shriek from Mam, a smothered laugh from Dad, a sharp 'Now Will' and a little chuckle from Mam herself. The girls sat up, saw candlelight shining under the door, jumped out of bed and peeped into the front bedroom. Dad stood in the flickering candlelight still wearing his boots and coat. Over by the window they could see the boys' faces through the painted bars of their bed. They had turned over, rolled up to their ears in the crumpled bedclothes and were peering out above the striped bolster. Dad chuckled again and moved to the foot of the bed. The girls looked in amazement. What was that lying beside Mam on the bed? An enormous feathered thing. Why it was a goose, a great big goose with its neck hanging over the side of the bed and its bill almost touching the floor. 'Now, Will, the lasses are awake as well,' said Mam from under the bedclothes. Somehow Dad was not properly ashamed of himself. He turned and held out his hands to his girls. They stood together and admired the goose. 'It were t'first prize,' he explained, then, with proper pride and ceremony, Dad raised its fat body from the bed and walked downstairs to pluck the monster. The girls looked at their mother and she shook her head.

The giant goose in all its glory re-appeared for Christmas dinner, after a week spent hanging naked on the workshop wall. There it sat, golden and glowing, on a huge blue and white dish borrowed expressly from the Post Office, surrounded by a steaming pile of brussels sprouts. Dad took up the carving knife, Grandad stroked his beard in anticipation, Mam and Grandma smoothed their skirts and took a sip of rhubarb wine and the girls passed their plates across the crocheted table-cloth. They ate until only a skeleton remained on the dish and their chins were greasy with the good meat. Dad retold the tale of his triumphant entry with due exaggeration. Then Mam capped it by swearing that when first she opened her eyes she thought Will had grown a long white beard overnight. 'Oh, Mam, you didn't,' all the children groaned.

The plum-pudding came on in flames and was followed by tea and mince pies. Even little Alan could hardly move after his dinner and had to sit still for at least five minutes. It was already dark outside. Firelight shone on the whole family crowded into the front room. It caught the white cloth on the table and reflected them all in facets and angles of the cut-glass knobs on the dresser against the wall. Only the piano remained black and silent, waiting until they had wind enough to unlock its keyboard and fill the room with carols.

8

Into Service

Nelly's last spring at school, the time for decisions about her future, arrived late with cold winds and high grey cloud. Sarah, peering with tired eyes, insisted more often 'What about our Nelly?' Bushman's usual and typical reply, 'Nay, I don't know,' was getting weaker as her twelfth birthday approached. 'She must go into service,' said Mam, 'Nelly's not big enough for t'mill.' She saw the problem in clear practical terms just as her own parents had done; at twelve years old children began to pay their own way and help their families. Life was hard and no one could afford sentimentality. One day they would move into the Post Office. Bushman would be postmaster and she could run the shop. Then their future would be assured. But after her years as a widow Sarah no longer quite trusted in promises of future happiness.

Nelly heard the words late at night or early in the morning, coming through the boarded bedroom floor from the kitchen below. She wrinkled her smooth forehead and, half elder sister, half little girl, put her arm round the dozing Annie beside her to comfort and be comforted. 'What's to be done with our Nelly?' The words echoed in her mind to the thump of Jack's clogs across the yard to collect his hammer from the workshop. It must be nearly six o'clock. Annie turned and muttered. Reuben's snore came through the wall. Even at seven he was a profound snorer, a loose and sleepy boy.

Jack vanished round the yard end. He had been at work now for more than three years, following his father, Harry Bell, into the quarry. No one could understand why Mam had allowed it after what had happened, but no one would say anything to question the decision. Between Dad's easy-going acceptance of the world, his unwillingness to push the children's futures in any way, and Mam's anxiety to bring in money and security, it was best to be quiet. Besides, a lad starting work at twelve did as he was told. Jack went to work at six o'clock on clear summer mornings. Bushman went with him the first day, down the village, past Mr Bond's rock house and the stables for the rock horses, along the side of the wood where it sloped down to the road and hid Quarry Hill. Just below them the quarry railway emerged from its tunnel to run over the sunken Old Road on a stone bridge and so down to the station in the valley.

The summer before he became a workman Jack and the girls had gone with long straws to collect wild strawberries under the trees and thread them together until the straws were hidden by a necklace of little red berries. Then they carried them home to be eaten with milk and sugar. They had called it 'Strawberry Hill'. When a file of dusty tired men came up past the quarry edge and down to the road, their work over, the children crept to watch them behind an elder bush, its stink close to their noses. As soon as the men had gone they peered out and bent down again to lift the delicate leaves, eager to fill their straws and be home.

Now, on Jack's first morning, Bushman and Jack, hammers over their shoulders, climbed past those elder bushes and along a grey cart-track rutted with dried mud. At its top, near the quarry workings, lay piles of huge rocks and here and there little heaps of broken stones. Other boys arrived and set to work. They laid their mats on the ground, squatted on their haunches, took a stone between their feet, and beat it to pieces with a two-pound double-ended hammer. 'Tha must make it just t'size of a pullet's egg,' they told

1. Thornton-in-Craven today seen from the valley and looking north towards the Pennine Hills. *(photo by David Richards)*

2. The village main road in 1900, with Billy-a-Doad standing by J. Wilkinson's fish and vegetable cart from Earby.

3. Thornton schoolchildren in 1889. Nelly Riley is on the extreme right, holding the hand of her brother Reuben.

4. Wright-Jack and his wife Hannah in retirement, 1909.

5. Four generations: Nelly, Bushman and Hannah Riley holding Nelly's first child.

6. The love tree as it is today. Love Tree Cottage is next to the Post Office, the building with the porch, and is still the home of Nelly Riley. *(photo by David Richards)*

7. Village children around the love tree in the 1900s.

8. Nelly Riley in 1976, aged 94. *(photo by David Richards)*

Jack, and winked at him behind Bushman's back. He knew them, every one. The work went on all day up there by the trees, in dusty sun or among damp autumn leaves. Take a stone, smash it into road-stone-size lumps, and then take another stone. The boys were paid by the size of their heap.

Bushman raised his sledge-hammer and easily and methodically he smashed up the big rocks with a few heavy blows. Then he left Jack, standing there with hammer and mat, to work through the day. At least Jack had a regular job, and the country another workman to build its roads. Nelly thought of him, just a lad, his steady round face and open mouth, singing like a choirboy down the road when the sun shone. Then she saw him as he came home covered in dust, weary and hot. She also would have to accept the job Mam chose for her, without complaint. She felt the fear of change tight in her stomach even as she lay still in bed.

A loud thump under the bed roused the girls. Mam was banging with the broom handle. Annie stirred and they reluctantly left their bed, pulled on their rough, black home-knitted stockings, and clattered down the steep stairs into the kitchen. Dad had lit the fire and water was heating in the boiler beside it. New flames flickered against the cold light from the window and just sharpened the damp air coming in through the open door. In a tight huddle, Alan in the middle, the children's sleepy bodies trotted across the yard to the earth closets. In the kitchen, flour porridge warmed over the fire and the skimmed milk, blue and cold, stood in a jug on the table. The children clattered back in and Mam's thin voice went right through them. 'There's coal to fetch, lads. Nelly and Annie, get them dishes washed!'

Reuben began moaning that he had a sore throat, croaking ostentatiously over his porridge. No one had much sympathy and, in readiness as for one last protest before school, Mam put a medium-sized potato in at the front of the fire. 'Right, school-time,' she said once the plates were cleared away. 'Me throat's too sore,' whispered Reuben. 'Mr Green'll be after thee,' said Alan, threatening Reuben with the fierce, red-haired truant officer. But Mam had everything prepared. 'Get me a sock, Nelly,' she said and, picking up the hot potato with the tongs, she stuffed it inside the sock and tied the poultice round Reuben's neck. Then he was sent out with the others, attached to his little packet of warmth. There was no easy escape from school.

Nelly had no thought of escape. She enjoyed both her school and the holidays, though Mam never liked to see her children with empty hands. Many a time Nelly had been lent to Billy-a-Doad's wife to help in the house and with her eight children, for there was plenty of work for a farmer's wife at Bell's Farm, whether out in the fields, looking after the cattle, trimming hedges or rebuilding the grey-stone walls around the fields. And in winter life was spent in the stone dark shippons, where cows were tethered to wooden posts, with damp stone flags underfoot and the warm, sweet smell of cow-muck and hay. Mrs Wilkinson, sharp and bustling, with small quick blue eyes, worked hard enough for two, and Billy-a-Doad sat contentedly in the kitchen, rocking the younger children on his knee.

Nelly was not kept very busy in that last Easter Holiday, when she was almost twelve. The Saturday before school began Mam could find nothing that cried out to be tidied, washed, mended, or looked after. Mabel Riley, her fair hair and thin face lit by bright spring sunshine, appeared at the door asking for Nelly. Sarah put the two girls in charge of a basket, some bread, butter, jam and the younger children, and sent them off on a picnic. They ran down the Old Road towards Elslack beck in the valley, leaving Mr Carr's villa behind, until they came to an enormous rugged stone bridge with embankments on either side of it. Up above, small solid horses plodded along in front of wagons of broken stone and a gloomy tunnel, cut into green meadows, led to the quarry deep in the hill above them. Nelly glimpsed the black tunnel entrance and wondered if Jack was about, perhaps even leading a horse through the dark.

Spoil heaps of grey rock, brightened by occasional fragments of white and discoloured marble, spilled out beyond the bridge. The lads began to scramble up the embankment, preparing to slide down the loose scree slopes, squatting on their clogs, daring each other to the steepest edges where rain had left hanging faces of dirt almost ready to fall. Nelly and Mabel screamed ineffectually at them to come down, for torn trousers would mean a thrashing. When they tired of the excitement the boys collected the brightest bits of marble to take home as treasures. They stopped to wash the finds in a small constrained waterfall which tumbled from the bridge out of a green pipe on to moss-covered stones and ran away in a cobbled gully towards the beck. This was the drain-pipe from the quarry workings. In winter it was fringed with long interwoven icicles.

The children ran quickly through the shadows of the bridge, hallooing at the echoes. Once safely in the open again Nelly and Mabel walked steadily, swinging the basket between them, but the boys rustled through the wet grass of the verges and kicked up showers of spray. Then they disappeared, off to the left-hand side, towards the beck and the great slab of stone which carried the path over to Elslack. In summer they would lie on their stomachs, flat on the cool stone, and watch minnows in the brown water beneath. Nelly called them back and they followed a green path across the little valley, through narrow, stone stiles beyond the railway embankments. Then they went up a steep hillside to the corner of Thornton wood, an overgrown plantation, its walls hung with great mounds and clumps of blackberry bushes, the long runners hiding fallen trees. Other visitors had beaten little paths between the bushes to get at the best berries, creating small enclosures, half overhung, and pleasant open sitting-rooms. Reuben and Alan chased off between the trees but the girls sat down on some fallen stones and looked across the valley towards their own village, now detached and distant, almost a painted scene.

Like miniature ladies, Nelly and Mabel sat upright, with knitting in their hands, in earnest conversation. 'Has your Mam found you a job, Nelly?' Mabel's face was full of concern, as she leant her head against her friend's dark hair. Nelly replied quietly, 'She's still thinking about it,' and began to brood a little herself. Annie bent over the ruined wall top, idly picking bluebells that had strayed out from under the trees. Then they all drew close together, for a rustling could be heard on the pathway. 'It's only t'lads,' said Annie nervously. 'Nay,' said Nelly, 'our Reuben couldn't be so quiet.' Mabel giggled and, as she fell silent, a white mongrel trotted confidently into the enclosure. 'Why, it's our Nettle.' 'She must have followed us all the way.' Mabel, abandoning her dignity for a second, growled most convincingly at her, and the dog looked up in surprise, cocked its head, then put a paw on her knee. They made a little couch for Nettle between them and fed her on bits of bread until the lads came back for dinner.

Children's time passes slowly but intensely, and with all the business of unpacking dinner, eating, playing with Nettle, and wandering home, they reached the love tree in good time for tea. Mabel turned towards her home as Nettle scampered in front and Annie and the lads scuffled behind. Outside their house stood a dark-blue dog cart. Inside sat a little grey terrier, looking about him like a solemn old gentleman, until he saw Nettle down by the wheel and begun to bark furiously over the edge. The Post Office door opened and a coachman's head peered out, with hair sleeked down for a formal visit, but with the splendid mutton-chop whiskers beyond control. 'Why, it's Mr Hutchinson.' 'Aye lass, Mrs Smith's in yonder with your Mam.' Then the coachman shouted 'Be quiet, you!' to the terrier, which ignored him, so Mr Hutchinson withdrew his head in disgust.

Pushing the lads in front of her and calling Nettle to come,

Nelly walked quickly round to the yard. 'What's happening, Dad?' 'It's Mrs Smith with your Mam. Better go in quietly.' The twisted sneck stuck, then rapped sharply in its hole. Mam heard them at once. 'Nelly, is that you?' 'Aye, Mam.' 'Come in here.' Nelly smoothed her pinafore, tugged her sleeves down to the wrist, and opened the door. She stood in the opening, her hands clasped, 'Come in, lass,' said Mam, 'Mrs Smith has a word to say.'

Mrs Smith sat, like her little dog, upright and self-possessed in grey, white lace at her throat. She smiled reassuringly at Nelly through round spectacles, then beckoned to her with a fine, smooth hand. Nelly walked over and stood beside her, one arm against the piano, touching its black side with the tips of her fingers. Mrs Smith took the other hand, cool flesh against warm, and smiled up at her again. 'Now, Ellen, your mother and I have been talking things over.' She paused and looked at Nelly appraisingly. Nelly gave a shaky smile and a nod in return. 'We think it might suit to have you come and work for me.' She paused again and Mam nodded agreement. 'Would you like that?' Nelly hesitated, and stood in silence until her Mam shook her head warningly. Nelly's voice was almost too soft to hear. 'Why, yes, I think so, ma'am.' What else could she say? 'Then I'll make all the arrangements with your mother.' Mam pointed to the door. Nelly turned and walked slowly out into the sunshine, not at all sure either of herself or her future, but compelled to accept both.

Annie came bouncing up to her, pestering with questions as soon as she was in the kitchen. Nelly, wanting to be alone, pushed her away and hurried across the yard to the garden, thankful to avoid the lads. She was not afraid of Mrs Smith, or of work, but she had never been away from home and needed time to get used to the idea. She must accept the place chosen for her, move to great Fence End House and work there as a domestic servant. It was a normal start to adult life, for she saw many servants about the village, cooks, maids, gardeners, coachmen, even governesses. Servants could make careers for themselves, just as her Mam had done, and rise to be cook in a big house on twenty pounds a year. Those village girls who were not sent to learn weaving in a mill generally had no other choice but to go into service. Even so, the last few weeks of school could only seem like a vanishing paradise. The fear of change was worse than change itself.

On a Sunday evening, only two weeks after the summer term had ended, Nelly packed her things for the first time in her life. She emptied her clothes from drawers and dresser and took down her shoes from the hook on the wall. It was all very strange, sad and formal, hard to believe that she was moving only half a mile away from home and yet leaving it all, house and people, behind her. She walked with her Dad down Thornton Drag in the evening sunlight, through the delicate shadows of ash leaves falling on the gravel. Dad carried her bag and gave her an arm. Nelly looked at the familiar hills and trees, at the railway below, at cows and meadows, but had no words to say. Bushman was a home-loving, comfortable man who had never ventured far from the Post Office where he was born. Perhaps he understood her feelings, even though he never objected to the pressures which put his children out to work. He squeezed her arm. 'It'll be all right, lass,' were his feeble words of comfort, 'tha knows Mary Hutchinson and her dad, and old Grace is a good sort.' Nelly gave him a heroic smile, and they walked on in silence until they came to the great stone house with its pillars and smooth, regular, façade, as upright, responsible, formal and unapproachable as Mrs Smith herself. Mrs Smith lived alone.

Bushman automatically ignored the pedimented front and took her round to the back door, in its angle between kitchen and dairy. Nelly stood beside him as he pulled the black bell chain, looking with interest at the signs of life, an old rose trained up the dairy wall and the scratches from animal claws below the door handle. There was a flapping of feet and a breathless, gruff woman's voice saying, 'I'm coming, I'm coming,' and the door was flung open. Old Grace, the cook, blocked the wide doorway, a round, loose shape in her print dress, slippers and mob cap, the grey hair curling out from underneath. But she smiled at Nelly, and signalled substantial kindness from bright blue eyes and sharp features half hidden by fat.

'Why, you'll be Nelly Riley. Come in, love,' and she turned, surprisingly quickly, to lead them inside. The kitchen, with its recessed windows and flagged floor, felt large and threatening, already gathering shadows in high corners as the evening darkened. Nelly stood, wide-eyed, looking at the room, half noticing the rows of copper pans, the china jelly moulds and the vast black cooking range, until Grace whirled round again. 'Right, lass, you sit down there, and I'll put the kettle on.' Then she turned again, 'And you'll be the famous Bushman Riley?' 'Aye,' said Bushman with a grin, as Grace took him by the elbow, dumped the bags by the door, and led him into the passage. There they had a muttered conversation, and when Grace's deep voice ended Nelly heard her Dad say 'Aye' once again. Grace had given him instructions, and he said goodbye quickly, would not stay for tea, kissed Nelly and went.

Grace and Nelly, left alone, had little to say, though Grace did her best, bustled over the tea and talked of the house and Mrs Smith. Soon Grace banged down her cup, rose up, and said, 'I'll show thee upstairs, come along lass; up the ladder and down the wall; pick up t'bags.' Nelly had to grin, just as her Dad had done. Grace responded with a sharp twinkle in her eye, 'Aye, Nelly Riley, so tha can smile,' and marched across the kitchen as she spoke.

The servants' bedroom was larger than Nelly's own little back-room at home. It had decent wallpaper, oilcloth on the floor, a chest of drawers and a dresser. Grace left her to settle in and put her things away. She sat on the edge of the big double bed, looking at Grace's few possessions, a hand mirror, blue enamel box of hair pins, two gilt fairings, a brown pot of cold cream. She thought of home as she undressed and climbed into that strange bed. There was no Annie wriggling beside her and whispering in her ear, no sound of Mam and Dad talking in low voices before the fire, no smell of coal, baking loaves, or crisp pies coming up the stairs, only the cold waxy smell of polished oilcloth from the long corridor leading to the front of the house. She turned over and over until her quiet tears wetted the lumpy pillow.

It was even worse when old Grace came up at ten o'clock. She was placid and calm, put her candle on the dresser and brushed out her hair. Then she sat down heavily on the edge of the bed and began to take off her stockings. Nelly lay tensely, breathing evenly, pretending to be asleep. Old Grace swung the bedclothes back and rolled into bed, turned over once or twice, and was soon snoring. Still Nelly did not dare to move. She held herself still, without a sound, keeping her misery to herself.

Next morning was bright and cheerful enough though Nelly felt tired and empty. She and Grace were up and about in the kitchen, starting the breakfast, Grace swinging pans on and off the range one-handed while she instructed Nelly in laying Mrs Smith's tray with the other. 'Napkin at the top, lass; that's better, we're all tidy here, except the cat.' Nelly, indeed, was tidy, and she let the cat in, for Grace had heard it scratching at the door. It was a splendid, big, kitchen tabby which walked in possessively, condescending to brush past Nelly's legs on its way to honour Grace with the full treatment. 'Polishing me slippers again, are you?' said Grace meltingly. Soon clean and straightened, they marched in to the dining-room for family prayers at eight o'clock. They stood quietly beside the table as Mrs Smith read a short passage. Then she put down the black Bible on the polished table, and sat waiting at its head, her fine hands folded. Grace and Nelly went out, finished preparing the breakfast, and brought in her tray.

They were never very busy in the big kitchen. Grace hummed to herself over the range, and as Nelly scoured the deep-bellied, steel hot-water pan, she would stop and look over its shining, rolled rim to the trees in the garden. The sunshine fell full against one dark cedar which stood in the lawns just clear of the house shadow. She could almost feel the light summer air moving its ponderous branches. She sighed and looked at the long black iron range. Grace wanted her to black-lead it tomorrow. She had never liked black leading, even on the fire at home. Her arms ached, her hands were filthy and she got dreadful smuts on her nose, But this afternoon, at least, Grace had promised to show her some of the special recipes she cooked for Mrs Smith's visitors. That would be fun; elaborate food they never attempted at home. Shrimp sauce, white soup, and angel's whispers, she wrote them carefully down in her own small recipe book. She began to sing, quietly but in a clear voice.

At night it was the same story as yesterday. She still missed her home, and lay in bed with her eyes open for two whole hours until Grace came up and she was forced to close them. They noticed. Mrs Smith saw her dark eyes in the morning and caught a sad little expression as Nelly carried in the breakfast tray. It was nothing obvious, Nelly wasn't making any fuss, but she had never had to learn to hide her feelings. Old Grace saw the tear-stained pillow and heard her sigh as she turned over at night. In the end she and Mrs Smith had a few words and Mrs Smith spoke to Nelly. 'Ellen, you don't seem to be settling here. Is there anything wrong?' 'No, Ma'am.' 'You do miss your home?' 'Yes, Ma'am.' There was nothing more to say and Nelly went off to the kitchen.

Nelly's first weeks in service settled into this regular pattern. Days were full of steady, light and unhurried work in a half empty house, from seven in the morning until eight at night. She helped in the kitchen, cleaned bedrooms and passages, opened the door to visitors, though still in her grey school dress and white pinafore. Sometimes she sang, but often she was too alone, left in some forgotten back bedroom with the mahogany chests and brown painted woodwork. Then, and especially at night, she felt deserted and comfortless.

Excitement and interest came from outside, from Thornton village, still lively and at work, half a mile up the road. Nelly would attend on the doorbell and generally find a tenant farmer, the rector or some other village personage, wanting to see Mrs Smith. They all said 'Hello, Nelly' as she stood beside the door. Village problems or tragedies were generally brought to Mrs Smith, who dealt with them in the detached, aristocratic way of those who grew up securely above them.

Nelly answered the doorbell one quiet afternoon, and stared in surprise at the black figure of her grandmother, in dark formal dress, bustle and all, planted determinedly between the pillars. This was an occasion, for Grandma's dignity rarely led her to call uninvited on her social superiors. 'Oh, Grandma,' said Nelly tearfully, for she had just spent a lonely half hour in the kitchen as Grace took a nap upstairs. But Grandma was too full of business to listen. She leaned over the doorstep and hissed, 'Has Miss Crowther been here?' 'No,' said Nelly in surprise. 'Right Nelly, I'd like to see Mrs Smith.' Grandma expanded a little, pulled her skirt round and reached up to pat her hair. 'But Grandma, she's gone out.' 'What!' said Grandma, who had dressed for the event and walked all the way from the Post Office. 'She went out about half an hour ago.' Grandma, who had come prepared to be angry, turned abruptly, then turned back, her dress rustling stiffly as she moved. 'I'll call again tomorrow, Nelly,' and she stalked indignantly down the steps without looking back, to march along the drive like a heavy black cloud on its way to a thunderstorm.

Nelly closed the door sadly. She would have loved to talk and confide in her Grandma. But now Grace was back in the kitchen, sitting and chopping vegetables for soup. She waved the knife at Nelly. 'Get that chin off the floor, lass. Who was it?' 'My Grandma.' 'Did she bring bad news?' 'She wanted to see Mrs Smith.' 'Well, no doubt that cat'll whisper the tale to us.' Grace winked over the knife blade, and Nelly laughed. But the cat was forestalled in its role of storyteller. Just as they were brewing tea Mary Hutchinson, the coachman's daughter, with the same shiny brown hair as her father and a pointing, inquisitive face came to the back door.

'Was that your Grandma at the front, Nelly?' 'Yes, it was.' So Mary took a chair and sat at the table end between them, then whispered, though no one else was about to hear, 'That poor Miss Crowther's opened a shop at Bar house.' Grace whistled. Nelly said 'Well, I never,' which she had just picked up from Grace. They thought of poor Miss Crowther, her soft eyes, untidy clothes and bastard son. Even with the lodgers she could never make ends meet. 'Your Grandma won't call her "poor Miss Crowther",' said Mary. Grandma Riley was known for her fierce opposition to any rival of her own shop, the source of independence and support. Grace chuckled: 'There's some wives in Thornton who don't call her "poor", either.' Nelly failed to blush at the thought, for she was a village girl, but at her age she had not the confidence to laugh out loud. Grace and Mary laughed, until Grace concluded, 'I wonder who'll be here first tomorrow?'

The next day was miserable, with persistent blowing rain; not a welcoming prospect for any petitioner who walked from the village to see Mrs Smith. Nelly ran, although she had been told not to, from the kitchen to the front door, as soon as she heard the bell. Sure enough, it was Grandma, furious and wet, her teeth tight together, grim white knuckles on the umbrella handle, and mud round the hem of her dress. 'Come in, Grandma. Are you all right . . . ?' Nelly's nervous talk stopped at a glance. Grandma sat down in the hall chair, looked down the corridor to see if anyone was about, not being pleased to use her grand-daughter as a go-between, then said, 'I must see Mrs Smith as soon as I can, Nelly.'

Nelly knocked on the drawing-room door, found Mrs Smith writing letters and asked, 'Can you see my Grandma now, please, Ma'am?' Mrs Smith frowned, just a little, before slowly folding the letter, closing her writing box, and following Nelly to the door. 'Come in, Mrs Riley,' she said, but, just as Grandma rose, the doorbell rang again and Nelly opened the door.

In her pink dress, her best, muddy for six inches or more and damp enough to cling to her softy body, Miss Crowther hesitated outside the door. Nelly looked in silence and it was Mrs Smith who spoke, efficiently but not kindly enough for Miss Crowther's misery, 'Please come in.' Rain and wind had freshened her face, bringing back the vanishing prettiness, the warm blood to round cheeks and curving chin. She moved as far as the doormat, to drip there, humbly anticipating defeat. The issue was business, survival, a part of the hard world of money and work; should Mrs Riley retain a shopping monopoly in Thornton? Sentiment and prettiness, perhaps even humanity, were at a discount. Grandma Riley, after one furious glance at the pink apparition, marched without hesitation into the drawing-room, so that Mrs Smith felt compelled to follow her. From that moment Miss Crowther's battle was lost.

Nelly, left alone in the hall with a damp woman, twice her age, a subject of sly fun in the village, was confused by surprise, some shame, human sympathy and an understanding of her family duty. She noticed the heavier stains of rain on the pink material, across the breasts, over the shoulders, under the arms. Why, the silly woman hadn't even brought an umbrella. Sympathy won and Nelly silently took her arm, led her to the chair and pushed her gently on to the seat. Then she retired, confused, to the kitchen where Grace and Mary were waiting.

They left the kitchen door open and sat in silence, listening at first only to Miss Crowther's occasional coughs and the creak of the hall chair as she moved uneasily. 'Well,

Nelly, what do you think of our Miss Crowther?' whispered Grace. 'Nay, I feel sorry for the poor woman,' Nelly replied softly. 'Right enough, lass, but you catch her looks when she's with a man. Makes you want to slap that silly face.' The drawing-room door opened. From the silent shadowy kitchen the three servants watched the drama. Miss Crowther stood up, face to face with Grandma Riley, black against pink. 'Mrs Riley . . .' she began, but Grandma raised her umbrella. As she spoke her voice was higher, less polished, the native hardness coming through: 'I'm not talking to thee. Get aside.' Then, glaring scornfully at the stained dress, 'There's muck enough hereabouts.' The umbrella came down, rapped hard on the flags, as she turned and marched to the door.

Grandma saw herself out, with a bang. Mrs Smith, her lips tight, looking her most aristocratic, paused then said, 'Now, Miss Crowther, what is all this about a shop? You rented Bar House as a home.' She pursed her lips again, then glanced down the hall and saw the open kitchen door. 'Come into the drawing-room.' Disappointment spread from Grace's face to Mary and Nelly. The story was only half told. Mrs Smith even saw Miss Crowther to the door herself. But Grandma Riley's victory was soon declared throughout the village. The shop at Bar House vanished overnight and Miss Crowther took in more lodgers, for which she earned more disapproval from respectable folk.

So the weeks passed by, and another Sunday came. Nelly still found it strange to dress in her Sunday clothes beside Grace. Stranger still to walk up the drag with her and to pass her own home without even stopping. She could imagine Alan's voice, 'There goes our Nelly,' and she wanted desperately to push inside and hug them all. When they came to church, of course, it was no family pew, but the servants' place beside the door. How could she bear it when her folk came in? After the first compulsive smile she bent her head to hide the misty tears in her eyes.

Grace was a kindly woman; she had tried with Nelly, had humoured her and given her time. Now she was prepared to speak her mind. After church she made her way to the sitting-room with a tray of tea, and when she had put it down, turned to Mrs Smith. 'I'd like a word with you, Ma'am.' 'Yes, Grace. What is it?' 'It's Ellen, Ma'am, you'll have to send her back home, she's fretting all the time.' Mrs Smith nodded thoughtfully, and suggested waiting a few more days. But Nelly got no better. Then the dog-cart was brought round again, bearing a message to Mrs Riley. Ellen was obviously not going to settle, could she be brought home?

Nelly felt a confused mixture of emotions as she walked back up the drag with her Dad under the shadow of the ash trees, not quite sure whether to be triumphant or ashamed. Dad smiled sympathetically at her every now and then. The family were in two minds. Was Nelly to be criticized for failing to earn her keep or quietly hugged because of her obvious love for home and family? One thing was clear for the future, whether they said it triumphantly or in desperation. 'Nelly won't settle away from home.' She was thrilled to be back and she put away her things in their old places, sat before the fire and went up to bed with her brothers and sisters just as she had always done.

Of course the news was all round the village. Nelly must have work, and good girls were hard to find. Soon Mrs Morris came down to see her Mam. 'Could Ellen come to help at the rectory for a few weeks?' Mrs Morris made it clear that Nelly would be able to live at home. There would be no such problems as at Fence End. Mam agreed at once, with a sigh over the difficulties of arranging her children's lives. Nelly could earn her keep, and she found things quite different at the rectory, for Mrs Morris was twenty years younger than her husband and there were children to fill the house. The older maids had admirers and were always getting into scrapes over it. They invented signals, wrote messages, and met on the back doorstep for a stolen half minute. And, of course, they were quite unable to keep it secret, but whispered the momentous news to every friend in the house as soon as anything happened, or might even be about to happen.

Nelly, in her turn, gave them the news of her own end of the village. 'You know Ella, the nursemaid at Mrs Carr's? Well, do you know, she's been meeting Harry Hewson in the evenings?' 'No, she hasn't?' 'Yes, she has, well, last night they were outside the back door, and suddenly there was such a row. Everybody by the Post Office heard it.' 'What happened?' 'There were all the children's heads sticking out of the window yelling "Oh, Mama, Harry's kissing Ella". You should have seen Ella's face!' All the maids collapsed in giggles at the very thought of being caught out in such a crime.

Not much later, they could all be seen peering round the corner of the servants' hall as Mrs Morris and her young brother-in-law, black eye-patch and all, came whooping down the long banisters with the children, laughing, screaming and running back up to the top to start again. Even a rector's wife could not be solemn for ever despite the need to keep up appearances before the servants and the village. The pressures of respectability were great, but not irresistible when challenged by such magnificent banisters. Suddenly, as she was half way round the circuit, the front door opened, and there stood Mr Morris himself, in full top-hat and breeches, fresh-faced from his ride. The little row of heads disappeared in an instant as he opened his mouth in surprise. Everyone froze. Would he be furious? Mr Morris had a temper when the occasion called for it. He looked quite sternly at the frozen group. Then slowly, at the sight of their anxious faces, his mouth turned upwards, he threw back his head and began to roar with laughter at the scene.

Every morning Nelly walked up the village to the rectory to begin cleaning and dusting. No little white cap and apron for her, like the living-in maids, for she was not expected to serve directly. Lunch, which they called dinner in the servants' hall, as Nelly did at home, was always the time when tales came out. The menservants, grooms and gardeners either went home to eat or brought a bait-box of food to open on their knees in the stables. They were not allowed inside, for by definition theirs was dirty work.

Nelly found it a pleasure to work inside the rectory. Delicate green and brown wallpapers covered the walls, fine carved tables and comfortable chairs filled the rooms. On sunny days they would hang out the washing in the yard and watch Mr Morris's horses being led out of the massive arched door of the stables. In the evenings, about four o'clock, the schoolchildren came to collect their quarts of skimmed milk and, as she scooped up milk from the vat to fill their cans, Nelly listened to their chatter, remembering them as infants at school in little skirts above podgy legs. Mrs Morris kept an eye on the maids but they all worked cheerfully enough. There was one problem to begin with, for she noticed that when Nelly Riley was cleaning the bedrooms, the chamber pots were never emptied, but left untouched in their elegant cupboards. Next day Mrs Morris called Nelly aside: 'Nelly, do you never look in those cupboards beside the beds?' Firm in her righteousness, Nelly replied, 'Oh no, Ma'am, my mother told me never to look in other people's cupboards, nor in drawers neither.'

9

Bushman's Battle

At haytime the sound of scythes being ground echoed round steep hill fields, while down in the valleys below the village, among the small water meadows, horses pulled mowing machines through dry grass. The brown, dried hay of the meadows lay in formal rows, marking them out from the green sheep fields of short cropped grass where good land ran up to intakes of the moor. Thornton remained a farming village, despite the modern activities which gave many folk work, a choice of income and more security and freedom. Whole families, such as the Hewsons, patriarchal father and married children, moved into vacant cottages in Thornton where they could be sure of work. When Mr Carr took on old Harry Hewson as his gardener the families he brought with him filled four two-roomed cottages down Station Road.

Thornton still needed help from all folk at haytime, and they came early from work, from the quarry, occasionally even from the mills, and always the schoolchildren lent a hand. It was no longer a question of whether there would be food to eat through the winter or whether the animals would live till spring, but the tradition remained.

Bushman, when he had finished repairing haycarts and hafting scythes, relished his long summer evenings in the hayfields. He enjoyed using all the strength of his body and feeling the muscles work in healthy rhythm. Most of his friends were farmers and they came to claim his help at different times. William Edmonson, tanned as far as his second shirt button, his rope-like neck turning at anything that attracted his bright grey eye, smiling as always, seized Bushman outside the Post Office. 'Bushman, th'art looking like a young cock . . .' 'Aye, I'll be there,' replied Bushman rapidly. He knew what William's compliment meant. 'Half past three?' He turned to go. 'Not wanting any ale then?' William's eyes twinkled to rival the Post Office doorknob. 'Oh,' said Bushman, as he stopped against the yard corner. William Edmonson gave him a moment to understand, then went on, 'I've a two-gallon keg in t'dairy. Bring it down with thee.' 'That I will,' replied Bushman. 'I'll be there.' William Edmonson chuckled, knowing he could rely on Bushman now.

Bushman arrived on time, making his way through the hot-smelling, fly-infested farmyard with a wooden keg over his shoulder, Nettle trotting at his feet. The hayfield was half full of children helping and playing, a few with wooden rakes, five or six perched high on the pile of untidy hay that almost filled William Edmonson's blue wagon. Bushman stood by the gate, hot in the sunshine, smelling dust from the hay and the strong sweat of horses tied in the shade under an elder tree nearby. 'Don't keep the flies off,' he thought, 'old wives' tale.' Bushman was a modern, progressive sceptic, and had no faith in the power of elder trees as insect repellent. Indeed the horses were flicking their ears, swishing their tails and puckering their skin against a swarm which seemed to have left the farm muck heap for choicer hunting grounds. A small foraging party flew over to inspect Bushman and he swatted idly at them, cursing, as he put the keg down. Then extravagantly, he stripped off his shirt, laid it over the keg and spoke to Nettle. 'Stay there. Look after t'beer,' and Nettle turned round three times before settling in the shade beside the keg. Bushman strode out towards the wagon, rippling his muscles, holding in his stomach, fortunately unaware of the fat whiteness of his skin.

The men working alongside William Edmonson, all in damp, stained shirts, grinned as Bushman came up, but none of them said anything. He took a fork and began passing hay on to the wagon. Sweat and grass dust collected on his skin and when he stopped to rest he shaded his eyes to look, past the dark summer green of the trees, towards the welcoming glint of water as Elslack Beck widened below the railway embankment.

A shout made them all turn. By the gate stood a thin figure waving a switch of elder over its head. Hartley Procter, limping a little as was usual, his face sallow, approached the work with caution. He stopped right in front of Bushman, wearing his stained shirt, an old tie baggily supporting his trousers and with a thin smile on his face. 'Bushman, tha should have been helping me.' 'Nay, I promised Will first.' 'Well, I'm on my own, a man can't make hay on his own.' This was true enough and Hartley Procter, who had moved from farm to farm always renting a smaller one, now attempted to run Chester Farm alone. He would claim Bushman's help whenever he could, leaning on him as a crony, persuading him out to the races or down to the pub when the farm could be left, or even when it should not have been left. Bushman could be led either way.

'Anyway,' said Hartley Procter, 'it's too bloody late to start now.' And, apparently in fun, he pushed the end of the elder stick into Bushman's fat navel. 'Hey, that's sharp.' Bushman put his hands to his stomach. 'Don't be so damn soft,' said Hartley Procter, and turning to William Edmonson, 'Were that a keg of beer I saw by t'gate?' 'Aye,' said William, glad to change the subject, 'tha can start it off for us.'

Hartley Procter limped back to the hedgeside while Bushman stood moodily watching, his hands still on his stomach. Hartley Procter reached for the beer keg, but Nettle must have felt her master's anger for she was up like a shot snarling and barking at Hartley Procter, running at his legs and outstretched hand until he was forced to defend himself with the elder stick. 'Yer bugger,' shouted Hartley Procter spitefully as he lashed at Nettle and she grew wilder. Then in disgust he stood back and shouted roughly above Nettle's continuous barking 'Hey, Bushman, call that bloody dog off.'

Bushman was still in the middle of the field, recovering his pride, so he grinned at the shouting, giving Hartley Procter time to wait and shout again. After a decent interval, drawing in his stomach, he walked slowly across the field and spoke commandingly, 'Get down, Nettle,' bending to pick up the keg himself. 'Reckon I'll take the first taste,' he said and raised the tap to his mouth. Hartley Procter, looking black as his own hair and eyes, said nothing, but shook his head when the keg was offered to him. All the other men had a drink, and a few of the lads too, but Hartley Procter loitered slowly away, beating the hedges with his switch.

In the last half hour of work they filled the wagon high and evenly. Then the horses were brought into the shafts and urged loudly to pull their weight until the wheels turned and the blue wagon creaked slowly up field into the farmyard. There the hay would be unloaded into William Edmonson's grey stone barn, with its narrow slit windows which let in dusty sunbeams to play over the heavy rafters. He and Bushman walked alongside, their forks on their shoulders, and to their surprise came upon the dark figure of Hartley Procter sitting on the dry stone wall beside the barn. He beckoned; they came over to him, and he spoke without apology or anger, for a bit of roughness either way was normal business. 'What dost tha say to t'pub tonight? It's been a hot day.' 'Not for me,' said William. 'There's work still to do.' Hartley Procter looked sharply at Bushman who had not spoken. 'I'll call for thee, Bushman.' Hartley Procter slid sideways over the wall and disappeared behind the barn.

Bushman came home for his tea smelling of beer and met a cold reception. The girls, recently persuaded to sign the pledge against alcohol, were going to a meeting that very evening. Their ridiculous flat white hats overshadowed the piano top. Bushman had bought the hats, and new white costumes too, after a celebrated win at the races. Even Mam had condoned this offence, allowing Bushman to take them all for a day trip to Morecambe. The memorial photograph, which showed a group of flat-faced statues in elaborate finery, now stood on the piano beside the hats. The girls were practising a few teetotal hymns. Annie plodded through the notes as Nelly sang sincerely the dreadful words of the songs. 'Father, dear Father, come home with me now.' Bushman found himself in a society which frowned on his little pleasures. Since the village pub had closed no one had been able to open another, and with the long walk to the neighbouring pubs Bushman really had little prospect of becoming a drunkard. Sober folk in Thornton had learned to disapprove even of men who liked their beer, and if they gambled as well, as Bushman did, their whole reputation was at risk.

Piano and voice ran on together. 'Come home, come home.' Bushman was saved from an awkward silence by a loud knocking at the door. Hartley Procter had the old silver-headed riding crop in his hand this time and poked a grinning yellow-toothed face around the jamb. 'Coming, Bushman?' 'Aye,' said Bushman. 'You're off to t'pub I suppose,' Sarah remarked coldly. Bushman, struggling into his jacket, was on his way to the door when Hartley Procter announced, loudly and maliciously, 'How much did tha lose at t'cock-fight last week, Bushman?' Sarah looked up sharply, angrily, as Bushman pushed his way clumsily out of the door, his arm still only half in his jacket. This was not only losing money, it meant illegality and a lost reputation as well. As soon as they were in the yard Bushman turned on Hartley Procter 'What the hell did tha say that for?' And Hartley Procter. chuckled. 'Th'art not scared of t'bloody women, art 'a? Come on, let's find Billy-a-Doad.' Bushman followed behind, fuming and sulky, his hands in his pockets.

Bushman's sulkiness vanished with the walk and the beer. Haymaking gave everyone a thirst, and quite a party of Thornton men gathered outside the pub to walk home together. Sunset was near. It was a warm evening with orange light reflected through streaks of cloud. They wandered along the beck, following each other by narrow paths among the nettles, catching the evening sounds of birds and the murmur of water beside them.

Hartley Procter stopped at a narrow stone stile, its two warm grey slabs set into the wall, just room enough to let a man's legs in, though it was a tight squeeze for Barrel Bradley. He was peering into the field beyond. 'Hist,' he said, 'what's that old ram doing? He's at the sheep at this time of night.' 'Beggar must have got out. He's at it all right,' Billy-a-Doad sniggered as he stood precariously on a loose stone. They stopped to watch, forming a line above the wall, a row of silhouettes against the orange-red sky. Barrel's great shoulders rose like a boulder built into the wall, topped by his heavy chin, and the small round close-cropped head above. He grunted with amusement. Frank Brown stood beside him, his quarryman's cape still slung over his shoulder, looking small by contrast. Bushman, laughing, his hands on the wall top, said admiringly, 'He's fair tupping.' Billy-a-Doad was still on his stone, and for once as tall as anyone, his curls black against the sky. Beside him Hartley Procter slouched against the stile, his head to one side, like an old gypsy, handkerchief around his neck. 'He don't choose 'em for their looks, does he? Bloody glad I'm not a shepherd,' and he nudged Billy-a-Doad almost off his stone. 'Give me Cissie Crowther any day.' It was all talk to Bushman; he shouted down the line, 'Does thy wife give thee Cissie Crowther then?'

Coldly, after half a second's thought, Hartley Procter threw it back to Bushman. 'Happen thy wife'll tell thee what she thinks about cockfighting, Bushman.' It had all been forgotten, even the anxiety about his homecoming, and a furious Bushman shouted, 'Shut thy face, it's nowt for thee.' Obviously the shot had stung him and Hartley Procter tried again: 'Bloody scared of his Sarah is our Bushman.' Bushman replied more furiously than ever, and with the ale inside him, 'If you bloody say owt more . . .' Whereupon Barrel laughed deeply beside him, and he shouted, 'And you shut up laughing.' Barrel, also with ale inside him, still chuckling, muttered, 'Can'st tha stop me?' Bushman, who could hear Hartley Procter laughing harshly in delight at widening the quarrel, turned in fury and struck the nearest opponent, Barrel, full in his stomach.

Barrel grunted with surprise and pain, his little eyes grew hard, and he turned to fight. They struggled out of their jackets and threw them against the wall, then took up positions in a clearing between the nettles and the stream bank. Barrel, true to his name stood stout and round, hands clenched in front of him, shoulder-of-mutton arms ready to pound like pistons, without skill but with solid weight. Bushman had read the sporting papers for years, had seen a a fight or two, and knew what was expected of a boxer. He took up his stance, one arm forward, one arm raised, and flexed his knees for action. 'Ready?' 'Aye.' Bushman struck, catching Barrel hard on his chin and drew back shaking his bruised knuckle. Barrel's pistons struck him hard on the cheek-bone and again hard on the shoulder. Bushman's right hand found Barrel's ear and made his head ring. Skill vanished, fighting began in earnest. Bushman slipped on a cowpat and fell on one knee. Their arms became entangled and they pushed and butted each other, breathing heavily. Barrel got an elbow in the ribs, Bushman an enormous fist in his gut. Bushman, moving faster, was more at risk from the uneven ground and slipped over the bank, flat on his stomach. He was up like a flash, shot over the edge, taking Barrel by surprise, and got him in the stomach with his head. Barrel staggered back against the wall.

The spectators scattered from their seats on the stones, giving room for the battle, but still yelling encouragement. The sheep, disturbed in their activities, had fled to the other side of the field and were bleating in anxiety. Hartley Procter's harsh voice, loud above the rest, told them to 'Get on with it.' Barrel shoved Bushman away. Bushman swung a fist sideways at Barrel's head. His cuff caught against the stones and came free after tearing half his shirt-sleeve away. Barrel's fist missed Bushman by inches, dislodging stones as he struck. Then they were tightly entangled again, butting with their heads.

Winded, the fighters stood looking at each other, their hands on their hips waiting to see who would move. The cheering had died down. It was quiet. Even the sheep were silent. Then, as Bushman began to move forward, a deep rich voice carried between them. 'Well, well, so it's Bushman and Barrel. I might have known.' The rector was looking down on them from the other side of the wall, high on the saddle of his horse. His red face bright in the sunset, billycock hat firm on his head. All their friends had vanished. Like two schoolboys in front of a schoolmaster, Barrel and Bushman hung their heads and turned away. They picked up their jackets and slunk off home side by side.

Bushman had no welcome from Sarah when he appeared in the lamplight, his face bruised, his shirt torn and his trousers filthy. She had sharp words prepared for him, but began, 'Oh, Will, are you all right?' When she found that he was and had dragged the story out, she attacked him with all the bitterness a responsible stay-at-home has for a vagabond. They went to bed in unhappy silence. Bushman snored heavily beside her and she lay awake worrying about what the rector might do. There were times when she had crept down with a candle while Bushman slept to check on the little pile of sovereigns he hid in the base of the American wall clock. It would be pointless that night, but they could not afford to lose either the money or their good name. Sarah suffered more than Bushman from his wildness. Anxious about the future, eager to inherit the security of the Post Office, she knew that the rector and Mrs Smith would be asked to recommend the next village postmaster. What if they turned against Bushman?

10

❧

Troubles at the Mill

'Did you know, Mrs Riley, that they're taking on folk at Bracewell's mill again?' 'Are they now,' said Sarah. Mrs Hartley, still self-important as in her cricket captain days, had sailed across the yard to catch her on the back doorstep. Now they stood upright on the cracked sandstone slab, symbols of respectability, never condescending, after all their years in the yard, to use Christian names. In silence for a moment, as the grindstone screeched in the workshop, they thought back over the troubles of that mill, down by the canal on the Thornton side of Barnoldswick.

The village had heard rumours of a strike and then more details of a lock-out. Everyone expected more disturbances, and one day Alan had rushed into the house shouting excitedly about soldiers in the village. Indeed a platoon of mounted troops could be seen, jingling through at a walk on steady horses, led by a fine young officer. They were proper soldiers in brightly coloured uniforms, for no one had thought of putting fighting men into grim khaki. The village women followed the little troop with their eyes as they walked their horses up the hill and vanished towards Barnoldswick. Then they went back inside to work. They could understand what the strikers were about, but it was a foolish thing to do, for it put a whole family's livelihood at risk on a single stroke.

Mrs Hartley and Mrs Riley shook their heads at each other in memory of that occasion. Their men would not be allowed to put the future at risk. Not if the women had any say in it. The children had come chattering back down the hill as the last bright glimpse of uniform disappeared behind the trees. News soon followed that the strikers had broken ranks and gone home without serious violence. Bracewell closed down his mill. All this was an echo of the old stories they had heard from the rough days when mills were first being built and bands of masked and desperate men, their whole living threatened, broke into buildings to smash the new spinning frames. Now the mills were solid realities and could not be driven away, or made to change the pattern they imposed, by such a small disturbance.

Mrs Hartley faced a hard world and relished the battles it brought her, taking full responsibility for her weak, asthmatic husband, the sickly boys and even the bouncing girls who took after their mother. When Mr Harrison took over the mill and reopened it, to weave cotton sheetings, Millie and Percy Hartley were sent to apply for jobs at once. Mr Harrison paid a good piece-work rate, at twenty-four yards to the piece, and a good girl could sometimes earn a pound a week. Since farmers' men in Thornton, with wives and children to support, only brought home ten shillings a week, the weavers' pay was good money. Mrs Hartley, the temptress, stood on the back doorstep of Love Tree Cottage, seeing herself as bringing blessings and not a curse. 'Don't let Nelly go up and down to t'rectory like that,' she said. 'Let her go to t'mill. Our Millie'll train her.'

Sarah thought of the money Nelly brought home every week, three shillings and sixpence for five and a half days at the rectory. In her mind it vanished beside the golden shine of that future sovereign. Would they ever be able to inherit the Post Office? Bushman's wildness put everything at risk, and she could not face poverty again now she was over forty. He should have had more sense, at his age. At least the children would do as they were told. She must be hard where she could. The decision was almost made. 'She'll not like the walking over to Barlick.' 'Why?' said Mrs Hartley, 'she can go with our lasses.' Sarah was already thinking about how to put it to Bushman and Nelly.

Almost, it seemed, a grim historical force pushed Nelly, as it had pushed thousands of others, from their countryside into the new dark, valley towns. Thornton on its green hillside, facing both east and west, was overlapped by the outer edges of two enormous economic regions, great textile empires which flooded the world with their goods. Thornton folk knew both of them; it was almost a question of which way you turned at the front door, west for cotton, east for wool.

Eastward in the Aire Valley, running through Yorkshire, lay a string of wool towns, weaving short-fibred wool and long-fibred worsted. A history of wool tied the whole countryside together: from the vast mediaeval sheep ranches of monasteries in the Craven Hills; through the fourteenth-century fulling mills and dyeshops of Skipton; the ever-increasing number of hand-looms in all the villages, as export of Yorkshire kerseys grew in volume; down to the new, powered, factories run on steam from Yorkshire coal.

Quite inevitably, so it seemed, this skill with wool had led on to the working of the foreign fibre, cotton. Cotton mills lined the Ribble Valley down in Lancashire, where folk worked up the yarn into cloth from bales of cotton brought in from America and Egypt. Mills had grown up like fungus in those damp valleys as the trade increased.

When Nelly asked her Grandma to tell of the old days, she spoke of the hand-loom weavers as she had seen them working the wool in their own homes. Once each little stone cottage had been a family factory. Children began to spin the thread as soon as they were old enough to be taught, and women took up their spindles from beside the bed as they rose in the morning. On spindles, unchanged for a thousand years, or spinning-wheels a mere two or three hundred years old, they pulled out the fibres, twisting them together, making strong and consistent yarn. The spinners could never let up, for all combined found it hard to produce enough to fill their father's loom, set before the window of the house, where he worked the treadles with his clogged feet and passed the shuttle to and fro by hand. There was a croft behind the cottage, space for an angled tenting frame to hold the cloth as it shrank and bleached in rain and sun. In those days it was a strange sight to travel through the stone villages and see white lengths of cloth standing out like flags against the grass on all the hillsides around the little rows of cottages.

Hand-loom weavers had to manage their own economy, to buy wool raw, card out the knots and tangled rubbish, comb it, spin it, weave it, and sell off the finished pieces. They might weave on commission and get credit for the raw wool. Always they kept a cow and grew vegetables on their land. They lived by their own hands and were responsible for their own work. It was a hard life, without security, and no family could afford illness or laziness.

In scattered villages and towns thousands of hand-loom weavers produced the millions of pieces of woollen Yorkshire kersey or finer cloths which sold throughout the kingdom and the world. Then changes had come thick and fast, in the times before Nelly's Grandma was born. The flying shuttle was mechanically driven through the shed of the loom, it cut out the hand-work and so made power looms possible. Then came spinning frames, jennies and mules, which at last solved the problem of producing enough spun yarn for the weavers. The spinning frames ran dozens of bobbins at once, put thousands out of work and caused riots when they were introduced.

Water power ran freely down the valleys, skilled workers could be had in plenty, and soon Watt's and others' steam engines would provide extra drive to the developing Industrial Revolution. It drew the folk out of their villages and down into the black mills. It drew the children too, now that they could no longer find useful work on the spinning-wheel. Nelly's Grandma could remember the hand-loom weavers at work, the wagons of wool merchants rumbling up the valley from Leeds, even pack-horses going over the top of the moors to Halifax, and the rolls of finished pieces stored in the great loft of Elm Tree House next to the love tree.

The mills were built and filled with machinery. A network of canals carried coal to drive them. Rows of houses were packed tightly beside the mills and up the steep sides of those narrow valleys to house the weavers, the spinners, the tacklers, donkeymen and overlookers. From all the villages around, folk who could have scratched only a risky, poor, living from the land, walked to the mills for the good money.

Nelly's journey to Harrison's mill was a logical result of this factory system. Her wages would be better than any hand-loom weaver could have expected. She would produce cheap, strong sheets for folk whose grandparents had slept under coarse blankets and had never known the comfort of good washable cotton underwear. Not that Nelly thought of such things, and they would have supplied a poor answer to a bright and growing girl of fourteen who asked why she must go to the mill. They brought no sparkle into her eye, nor made her burst into song on her way.

Nelly was afraid of it all. She saw the mill buildings whenever she went into town, like great prisons with high grim walls and no windows, and the strange, dirty-faced, half-naked men, chewing tobacco, who shovelled coal into the thundering engines beside their enormous chimneys. They poured out black clouds of smoke which fell heavily on the ranks of houses drawn up beside them. Every morning their shrieking whistles summoned sleepy crowds inside the dark, wide doors where steam rose in clouds and the thunder of heavy machinery echoed into the empty streets.

That first morning it was hard enough getting up at a quarter to five from the warm bed, but to see Annie still lying there in a heap of bedclothes, after having opened one eye and closed it again as she settled down for another two hours, was almost more than Nelly could bear. It was a greyish overcast day outside and her fingers felt thick and clumsy as she fastened her buttons, pulled on her stockings, and went downstairs. She did not even feel like the tea and bread and butter that her mother had got ready for her, but set off on time with the Hartley girls, her eyes big and solemn, her hair tied back, to keep it clear of the looms.

It was the same every day for weeks and months on end. Each morning, through two long winters, they plodded along the cold, dripping road, for it was too dark to see the way over the fields. When rain poured down the girls drew their cloaks and heavy skirts round them and splashed through the puddles in their good, wooden-soled clogs. On those days Nelly took a can of cold tea and hooked it over the edge of the bubbling vat of water beside the engine-room to warm itself and then her. At the end of the day she had to face the long walk home to the fireside and her family. At least in winter, when the mill rose up in the darkness to meet them and the shed door was open, they could feel pleasure in the warm air pouring out and the light from gas mantles along the walls. It was best on crisp autumn days, when the frost lay thick on the path across the fields and even the clammy weaving shed took all morning to drive the roses from their cheeks.

So too in spring, after the second winter, when they could at last see the field path again and no longer had to grope past clammy hedgerows, the five o'clock start was easier to accept. Other lasses would sing their way downhill, or scamper with lads, for they were only fifteen or sixteen and had the remains of childhood still to use. Nelly generally kept quiet, thinking of the book she was reading at home in the peaceful evenings, saving her strength for the day. Spring lengthened into summer and the black mill became more of a threat each morning when it appeared against the sunlit hills as Thornton disappeared below them. She felt more tired every day. Mam began to notice how listless and pale her lass had become, often climbing upstairs to bed well before the lads, who were still at school. Sarah dismissed Nelly's weakness as growing pains. After all, she would soon be a woman. But Nelly's weakness dragged on for months.

One summer's day Nelly pulled herself out of bed and looked at the faint red glow in a white sky. It had been close all night, there was thunder about and she had slept badly. Now the dawn felt cool and still and she would gladly have turned back to the bed and slept for hours. The sun was hidden behind Quarry Hill but it shone along the brown tops of the moors, and the sky, lit from below, seemed higher than ever. She pulled on her cotton summer dress, folded up her apron, and decided not to walk in it that day but just put on her coat, for it was going to be hot. Then, rubbing her eyes and shaking her head in an effort to clear it, she walked downstairs, sat on a chair and put on her clogs. She did not bother with tea but had a cup of skimmed milk and a slice of bread and butter. In her basket she put a jam pasty, two slices of bread and butter, and her apron. That would last her until she came back home for dinner.

She washed her face at the sink, hung her coat·round her shoulders, looked at the clock, and opened the back door. As she came round the corner of the yard she could see Ned, Percy, Mary and Millie Hartley down by the love tree, sitting quietly for a second on the cool stone seat. A thrush was singing in Mr Carr's garden. The rooks had already left home and were noisily settling in the fields beyond Thornton Hall Farm. As they went up the village odd doors opened, cattle could be heard moving in the shippons and Mrs Maiden, a left-handed woman with a left-handed tongue, peeped out quickly, looked suspiciously at them, and slammed the door again before they went past.

From the top of Thornton hill they could see the sun already half-way down the moors and beginning to shine round the corner of Quarry Hill towards the village. They kicked up no dust on the gravel road, for it was still bound in by the night's dew. It was cool and pleasant under the trees' shade, a temptation to stroll and talk, but they all knew they had to be standing beside their looms at six o'clock. They hurried down the road to the church, Millie chattering, the boys running into the verges now and then, and Nelly, still a little drowsy, following along beside Mary.

At Nutter Cote Farm they cut across the end of Swilber Hill leaving the winding road below them. The grass was still wet for they were in the cool shadow of the hill, and the wide valley beyond, stretching towards the forest of Bowland, was marked with long shadows and bright patches of sunlight. Plovers rose from the grass and piped at them, while a few lonely cows began to gather together and hopefully followed the little group along the footpath until they reached the stone stile by Ghyll church.

As they came round the corner they could look down towards the mill. A shining curve of canal swept round the hillside and passed beside the weaving shed. The great stone building under its slate roof was set against a green countryside of trees and hills. It looked unnatural, even unreal, in the clear morning sunshine, so heavy, still, and silent, as birds sang above the lane that led towards it. Just beyond its entrance gate the road crossed over into Barnoldswick by a hump-backed bridge and beside it stood two tiny stone cottages. Behind them lay the yard where barges unloaded coal for the furnaces. Black smoke, already oozing lazily from the chimney top, was casting miniature cloud shadows and now the sun shone fully on mounds of black shining coal beside the boiler house, catching flecks of crystal in the grey millstone of the high shed walls. The girls walked on to the road and then into the cobbled yard to join other groups of clogs before the shadows of the mill door swallowed them up.

Nelly felt the close, damp, warm air of the weaving shed

wrap around her. The cotton fibres depended on this peculiar climate, but it did not suit her. She put down her basket, hung up her coat and smoothed her apron into place, then went mechanically and quietly to stand beside her row of looms. Norcross Harrison, over-looker and tackler, with grease already on his hands and arms, peered along the black row of machines and nodded. No one spoke much in the shed, it was no use when the looms were going, and the girls soon learnt to lip-read. Then came noises from the engine-room. Great black oily shafts, fixed to solid pad-stones along the walls, began to rumble. Leather belts lashed to and fro and then pulled steadily as the looms started up. Noise went through Nelly's head as soon as work began that day. It was all she could do to walk up the row and seem to be inspecting her looms.

At each pick of the loom the brass, bullet-ended, wooden shuttle was smashed forward on its short journey across the shed, to be stopped dead at the other end and smashed back again. The warp moved steadily forward, healds and reeds rising and falling as the piece of material gradually fattened on its great roll below. The solid black cast-iron Lancashire looms were in full action, the result of half a century's improvement and producing, in the hands of young girls like Nelly, as much cloth in a day as a hand-loom weaver had turned out in a week. The third loom had stopped and Nelly picked up the shuttle to replace the empty cop with one full of yarn. She placed it in its slot and fed the yarn end into the running groove. As she bent over to kiss the shuttle and pull out the yarn with her teeth, the noise in her head roared louder, her eyes closed and she leaned forward against the cold iron column beside her for a moment. It passed over. She carried on until eight-thirty when they stopped for ten minutes and had a bite to eat.

Nelly stood by her loom and ate a slice of bread and butter. The sun was high outside and through smears in the white-washed windows she could see blue sky above the saw-tooth roof, though no sunlight ever came into the shed. Now and then the shadow of a heavy cloud passed by. It was oppressive and stuffy that day and already she could feel her clothes sticking to her. Her palms were damp and her head ached with a steady beat. The looms were off again and the noise rose around her. As the day grew steadily hotter everyone was wet. Sweat soaked the light cotton of their dresses, and the tacklers, bending over their looms, wiped their foreheads time after time so that grease steadily passed on to their faces until they were a shining pattern of black and white.

Nelly never knew how she carried on till lunchtime, but it was like paradise to walk out into the sunshine of the mill yard, to see sunlight on the canal water, and to buy a pot of home-made lemonade from Mrs Anderson in her cottage. The girls sat in the long grass of the canal bank, held brown stoneware mugs between their hands and drank in gulps. The boys walked along the towpath and threw stones into the water. Nelly lay back in the long grass and closed her eyes, listening to the splashes and the distant noises. Sunlight shone in a red glow through her eyelids and she pulled the apron over her head as a shield. Stalks of fresh grass flattened beneath her head. She was content to lie still, careless about the tangles in her hair, not even wanting to eat her pasty or nibble at the bread and butter. Quietly she drifted into sleep.

The whistle went, close by and shrill, transmitting a flash of pain through Nelly's aching head. She could only have slept for a few moments. The sun was still hot and high as she pulled the apron down, narrowing her eyes to face the glare. Millie and the others were already in the yard. She rolled over and dragged herself to her feet, feeling empty in head and body, clammy, with heavy, aching limbs. The weaving shed filled again with a thunder of looms and thick, damp, air. An hour passed since lunchtime. Only three more long hours to go, as the oppressive heat increased all afternoon.

She looked quickly round at the long shed behind her.

The flags, shiny with oil, reflected patches of yellow light along the alleys between looms. Among the black machines she could see grey figures bending over their work, all except Mrs Shuttleworth who leant against the iron column behind her, dress hem filthy from the floor, stains across the front of her blouse. She was chewing tobacco again. How Nelly hated them, the coarseness and crude language. She could see the old married couples here and there, some of them over seventy, running their eight looms together. They began at six in the morning, winter and summer, just as she did, and had been doing so for sixty years. They had no alternative but work for an independent old age. They bent to the looms as if made for it, quiet slow-speaking folk who saved their energies for the walk home.

The roar from the ranks of heavy iron looms crowded together seemed to be shaking her to pieces. Her eyes swam, and the shapes of the machines seemed to change and move as if a herd of enormous animals crouched there for shelter. Nelly bent over, tied in a broken end, and then looked quickly up at the clock. Two more hours were left. She stooped again, for the thousandth time, finding another broken end. She felt a drumming inside her head, darkness and noise filled her brain entirely. Silently she fell down beside the loom.

She opened her eyes to dreamlike uncertainty. Nothing in view was familiar to her at all and soft, lumpy, objects were underneath her. She had no curiosity, no desire to move her head and see more. Then a face appeared, upside down and not easy to read. For a moment she puzzled then whispered 'Mr Harrison.' 'Aye, lass,' he said kindly, 'now lie still, I've sent for t'doctor.' Nelly made no sense of the talking around her, or the stir as folk were sent back to work. It was a blessing to close her eyes again, and for some time she lay in quiet. She must be in the warehouse among cotton bales, for the distant rumble of looms could still be heard. Then a voice said 'Nelly', and she opened her eyes to see, against the iron frame of the roof, the anxious face and drooping moustache of her Dad.

Bushman picked her up, carried her outside in her stained cotton dress, and lifted her into Mr Carr's waiting dog-cart. There she lay on the leather seat and watched, through half-closed eyes, as the black finger of the mill chimney slowly shrank behind the hill, until it disappeared entirely when they passed under the green shade of trees. Then she could close her eyes and feel, through the bones of her head, the peaceful sound of horses' hooves on dry gravel and the regular creak of the cart's wooden joints.

Mam put her to bed. The doctor, having ridden alongside the dog-cart, saw her settled, prescribed a tonic and left. Nelly found time most uncertain, but noticed dark clouds gather and heard the first sticky drops of rain on the slates above her. Then it poured.

11

School at Salterforth

Nelly was allowed downstairs next morning, wrapped in a shawl, after the family had gone to work. Everything was still, no looms, no clattering clogs, no hot, damp air or steady rumble from the drive-shafts in the weaving shed. She sat quietly with her eyes closed. Mam was sewing in the front room, humming to herself. Grandma came in from the shop. 'Morning, Sarah, how's our Ellen?' she said. 'She's in t'kitchen by t'fire. Doctor said we could let her down for a while.' Grandma walked through and stood in the doorway beside the tall, brown-painted dresser with its row of tins, caddies, and bowls. She had put no cap on just to pop round the corner, but her black bodice was buttoned right up, the lace carefully pinned at her neck. 'Hello, Grandma,' said Nelly, and smiled half-tearfully, for her grandmother, she knew, was on her side in this. The old lady stood beside Nelly and put a hand on her head. In a quiet voice, so as not to be heard in the front room, she said 'Nay, Ellen, I'm right suited. Let's see if this'll end it. I never liked thee going to t'mill.' Nelly had never seen her grandmother quite so conspiratorial. She reached up to take her hand and whispered, 'I don't want to go back, Grandma.' From her pocket Grandma brought out a little triangular bag. 'I've some spice for thee,' she said more loudly, and opened the packet. 'It's best Harrogate toffee.' Then she felt Nelly's forehead and told her that she didn't look that bad, before leaving by the back door. It was generally agreed that Nelly should be spoiled a little. Dad came in later and told her as much with a wink and a nod.

Nelly lived on a diet of milk and eggs. Mam had been hard on the lass, had sent her to the mill against grandmother's open objections and grandfather and Bushman's silent disapproval. She had expected no more from Nelly than she did from herself: a lifetime of continuous work. Now she accepted her mistake, she made no apologies, but, like all Mam's enterprises, the job of making Nelly better was to be done properly. Jack went round to Thornton Hall Farm after work to bring home an enamel milk kit full of creamy milk. There would be no blue skim milk from the rectory; a milk diet meant real thick yellow milk. At times it was almost too rich to drink. 'Now, Nelly, get it down, it'll do thee good,' and she was left with a greasy moustache over her mouth. Mam brought in the mirror from her bedroom and they both laughed at it.

The days ran on into weeks and she could see from her bedroom window the sun shining, first on green and then on the golden-brown of drying hay. As she lay in her bed her eyes moved over the bright patterns of her counterpane and her fingers traced the separate squares sewn together by her Mam when she was a little girl. She lay and watched the light change on the hills and listened to the regular noises from the yard. Sometimes, if her eyes opened early enough in the morning, she would catch the Hartleys slamming their door, hear Millie's voice above the rest and know that they were off to the mill along the old unhappy way. Then she stretched in delight and closed her eyes to shut out thoughts of the weaving shed. The fear was still there, for when she was better must it not all begin again? The family needed money and what else could she do? How long would her time of peace last?

They were cutting the hay and the hill turned brown with stubble. The yard filled with carts, creaking in and out, snorting horses, stamping of feet and shouts from the workshop. Dad was busy all day, his face brown and cheerful, and in the evenings, when he could, he was out in the hayfields. As Nelly improved they let her out on warm afternoons to walk into the hayfields herself and sit in the sun under a hedgerow. She watched the children tossing hay in the air, climbing on to the wagon-loads and jumping off into the soft piles below, and when they tired a little they would come shyly over to her. 'Hello, Nelly' or 'Miss Riley' sometimes. Little girls would sit beside her in the warm dry grass and show her the limp handfuls of flowers gathered in the heat of the sun, or baggy dolls in their tattered old clothes, worn out by the long months of play since Christmas. Nelly looked and admired and soon it was 'Tell us a tale'. She searched through her memories of stories read and heard, from the Arabian Nights to Robin Hood. Most of all they seemed to love the sad little stories of orphan children and cold winter nights, Babes in the Wood or Hansel and Gretel. These filled them with delightful sadness. The children moved closely round her, sitting on the edge of her skirt.

She had been at home for two months when the doctor called for the last time. He seemed pleased with her progress, felt her forehead, examined her eyes, took her pulse, and went down to talk to Mam. Nelly lay still again, heard the voices downstairs and was curious to know what was said. She slid out of bed and in bare feet crept down the stairs. The doctor stood at the open door on his way out. She could see his horse tied up outside the Post Office. Then the door closed behind him. 'Mam, what did he say?' Mam put her arm round Nelly's shoulders. Dad was standing beside her and took her hand. 'We've been talking it over, lass. Doctor thinks you're not fit for t'mill again. There's no need to go back,' said Dad. Nelly's face brightened 'Oh, Mam,' she said, 'but what shall I do?' 'Get better first, then we'll think on it.'

Now the time could pass by easily without hidden worry.

Soon Nelly was downstairs and busy about the house, eating her hash and solid foods; parkin, pasties and roast meat. The skimmed milk gradually re-appeared, driving out its richer rival. Nelly began to help, to take on the cooking and cleaning to leave Mam more time for dressmaking. It was pleasant to have time. Not to have to work at the demanding pace of those great black looms. Now she herself decided when the oven was ready for the bread or the stew, and if she wanted to walk up to the garden for a few more carrots or onions, the oven would wait for her.

On bright winter mornings, when Annie, now in service herself, had got up and gone downstairs, Nelly could lie in bed for a few delightful moments as cool light poured into the room, wriggle her toes and dream, waiting for the schoolboys to leave. When they had gone she went downstairs and washed the breakfast pots, rubbed soap on shirt collars and cuffs and put them into the dolly-tub to soak. Then she could take a long walk up the lane by Mrs Hartley's, towards Wilson's Fold and over the hilltop behind Thornton. She cut down through the water meadows, clambered along the little green steps of the sheep runs which edged across the hillsides, until she reached Crickle Beck. It was cold and clear that winter, with a white sun, and frost clinging to the rushes by the banks of the stream. She followed it a little, then, by Shed Laithe barn, leant against an old birch tree and stood still until she could feel the quietness around her. It was like being a child again to have all this time. She picked up a smooth frosty stone from beside the beck, played with it, and dropped it into the dark rushing water.

Her mother looked up and smiled when Nelly came back into the house with bright eyes, healthy cheeks and a few sprays of early catkin in her hands. She had been wrong to send Nelly to the mill. She turned to Nelly's Aunt Lizzie, who sat beside her in the front room methodically sewing on buttons. 'I don't know what to do with our Nelly. Folk keep coming round and saying "can Nelly come and help me a bit". She goes round to Mrs Wilkinson's now and again and she's always called on for a lying-in.'

Aunt Lizzie was a self-appointed lady, youngest daughter at the Post Office and not yet thirty. She was tough, selfish, and as determined to keep up the family position as Grandma. Aunt Lizzie had a wide social circle and many acquaintances though no one had yet been induced to ask her hand in marriage. Obviously she had a plan. 'Nelly's done quite well at school, hasn't she, Sarah?' 'Aye, she finished standard six, and Mr Lambert had her looking after the babies for a year or more.' 'She's always reading?' 'Aye Lizzie, do you know I found her about harvest time with a right flock of babies just out of school, and she were telling them a story.'

After a while Aunt Lizzie spoke thoughtfully. 'I've told thee about Ralph Longtoft and his sister at Salterforth.' 'Aye.' 'Well, he's schoolmaster there down by t'canal. I went over there to tea, it'd be two weeks ago, and he told me he's looking for a new helper.' Another pause for button-holing. 'Do you think our Nelly might like it?' 'Well,' said Mam, 'we can but try, it wouldn't be hard work like t'mill.' 'I shall be seeing the Longtofts on Saturday, Sarah, and I'll talk to Ralph about our Nelly. Don't say anything to her yet.'

On Monday morning Mam called Nelly into the front room and told her to sit down by the fire while she and Aunt Lizzie worked. They had a few quiet words and then Mam said, 'Now, Nelly, have you given thought to what you'd like to do?' Nelly sat still, holding her knees, and shook her head thoughtfully. Aunt Lizzie grunted disapprovingly. Of course, Nelly had been thinking and worrying, but she had very little idea of what could be done and not much confidence at the moment that she could do it. She was seventeen now and grown up, slim, with long rich dark hair that could be curled into ringlets and shone a red-brown in the light. Her quiet determination, the capacity to manage situations, remained half hidden even to her watching mother. The surprising gaiety, the helpless bursts of infectious laughter which suddenly exploded out of her quiet, had become rare things in her time at the mill.

She looked thoughtfully at the fire, while Mam put down the half-finished dress and concentrated on what she had to say. Nelly was surprised and interested in the idea of working at a school. It was a world she knew about, with happy memories of Thornton school mixed with the Christmas parties Mr Carr gave to all the children, and her last year, when she had shown all the wide-eyed babies their presents from around the tree. Mam finished her tale and Aunt Lizzie capped it at once. Nelly could go to Salterforth and speak to Ralph Longtoft on Wednesday at lunchtime. Mother said, 'It's come just at the right time. Do you think you can walk over to Salterforth?' and Nelly said, 'I'll manage.'

She lay awake on Tuesday night, going over all the things she had learnt and forgotten at school and wondering what Mr Longtoft would be like. Next morning, as she looked down from the hills on to the little huddled roofs in their narrow valley, and saw the stone schoolroom beyond them, she wondered again. She had never been interviewed before and her mind ran over all kinds of possible scenes in which Mr Longtoft varied between an ogre and an angel. Mrs Smith had known her all her life and her family before that. At the mill Mr Harrison had spoken a gruff word about 'Learning t'job' and 'keeping to it' and that was that. Nelly had been too frightened to listen. Now she must convince that unknown schoolmaster that she could be a good helper. She could write a clear hand, read well, do simple sums. She was interested in history and geography. Would that be enough?

She grew more nervous as she came downhill through the twisted streets of Salterforth, among puddles and stone setts, then passed a field and a pub to the schoolhouse. She hesitated at the gate, then went through and walked up to the arched doorway. There she knocked boldly and, opening the door a crack, looked inside. Mr Longtoft was present, bustling around the class-room. He came over at once and looked at her with twinkling eyes. 'Ah, you'll be Miss Riley. I won't be a moment.' Nelly stood in the doorway as he trotted over to his desk, collected an exercise book, and trotted back again. 'Now,' he said, 'to business.' Nelly smiled nervously and Mr Longtoft smiled back. He was a slim small man, light on his feet, running off to look out of the door and then running back to her with a 'Sorry, Miss Riley, you'll understand I have to keep an eye on them.' He had a fast, moving face too, a mouth that drew the words as he spoke, and brown eyes that flickered over his listener's face, then off round the room like a pair of birds. She could hardly help liking him at once. After a brief talk, a walk around the school, and a few brisk trots into the playground, he stopped and looked her straight in the face. 'Oh yes, I think you'll do,' and that was that.

Her interview was almost alarmingly rapid. 'We must get the rector's approval. I'll drop you a note to let you know when to call on him. Will you be able to go and see him?' Nelly nodded. 'Good. Can you start next month?' Nelly needed a short pause to catch up although she wasn't at all uncertain. 'Yes, I think so.' 'Very well, Miss Riley, I'll be pleased to see you then. Give my regards to your aunt.' And he was off into the school again. Nelly stood for a moment in fitful sunlight, looking at the small schoolhouse without seeing anything at all. She had to walk slowly home, to have time for thinking over all that had happened and understanding what it meant. Could she really believe her eyes and ears? But the note came, and she called on the rector of Barnoldswick, who asked her serious questions about her up-bringing and revealed that he had spoken to Mr Morris. He too said, 'Yes, you'll do,' and as Nelly still remarks: 'So I did.'

As the next month approached Nelly took down her old

schoolbooks, washed and ironed white blouses and carefully pressed her two dark skirts. Then she took her sandwiches and books up Thornton hill and straight on over the green hill towards her school. Miss Riley was put in charge of the babies' class and soon felt quite at home. As she walked over the fields each morning there would be little figures waiting at lane ends, small grinning faces peering round wall corners, waiting to rush out and grab her hand or at least a corner of her skirt. She would arrive at school surrounded by a busy, clamouring crowd, like a mother hen with a large family.

When the whistle went they all gathered in Mr Long-toft's classroom and he said the prayers. Miss Riley stood behind the class and saw that the babies were quiet. Then it was squeaking slate pencils, dusty slates and chubby hands to be guided over their letters. Someone was always calling for Miss Riley to help them. Soon she knew all the children, and their brothers and sisters too, when they came along. The children talked away and Nelly listened and observed. Soon she knew all about them and their lives, which were generally cheerful and full of life but sometimes truly sad.

Little Alice, the butcher's daughter, with round, rosy cheeks felt ill and stayed away from school. Mr Longtoft told Nelly gravely that it was meningitis, and for once he walked soberly off to the front of the class with a long face and a long stride. Nelly thought sadly, as she piled up lesson-books against the painted panelling, of the cheerful, noisy baby she had tapped on the head time and again, telling her to be quiet. Later that week Alice's mother appeared at school, a worried, dumpy, straggly-haired woman. She spoke to Mr Longtoft, and as he led her over to Nelly she began to talk on the way. 'Miss Riley, it's our Alice. She's got such a fever, and now she's taken it into her head to say some poetry. She goes over it and over it, and we can't make her stop and she never can remember it all. She keeps saying,

"I wish Miss Riley was here".' The poor stout woman had dark rings about her eyes. She repeated her story again, almost word for word, obviously unable to think about anything beyond Alice's urgent need. Nelly opened her mouth with no idea what reply to make, but Mr Longtoft looked at her and spoke first. 'You'd better go at once.' Nelly nodded, said, 'Yes I'll come,' put on her cape, and followed Alice's mother along the narrow street to the house behind the shop.

Alice lay among huddled bedclothes in the big bed she shared with two sisters. Signs of illness disturbed this children's bedroom. Brown and green medicine bottles, a chamber-pot still standing on the oilcloth, a jug of water and the dried remnants of wet poultices, all drove the dolls and toys away into remote corners. Nelly looked at the sad pale face among the pillows and took hold of her hand. Alice opened her eyes slowly. 'Oh, Miss Riley,' she said, and began at once to go through her favourite poem. She spoke in an odd, mechanical way and in a croaking voice until, almost at the end, her mind failed her. Her whispering voice repeated a line again and again, so that Nelly had to bend over the bed to catch the words. She took up the sounds, slowly and carefully, carrying Alice along with her, until together they finished. Alice gave a little contented smile, her frown disappeared, and she stopped murmuring the words. As Nelly stood beside the bed, having done the one thing that was in her power, the child fell asleep. Her mother sighed and looked ready to burst into tears.

Nelly refused a cup of tea, not quite understanding that Alice's mother had wanted her company rather than refreshment. Nelly was glad to escape and set off sadly back to school. Of course the doctors could do nothing, less perhaps than Nelly or Alice's mother. The whole school went to Alice's funeral and six of the boys carried her coffin to the graveside. The children were not often given a holiday to go to a funeral, although most had tales of friends, brothers, or sisters who died and would have soon been forgotten but for the recollections of their parents by the fireside.

They were always busy in the class-room, and Nelly now had full responsibility for the babies. Mr Longtoft told her clearly that he expected his assistants to train and become fully-qualified teachers. 'I don't like to take anyone on unless they're keen to learn.' Nelly was keen enough, though she found it hard at times. She was paid three pounds a month salary, and given the expenses of her training. Mam couldn't complain about her contribution and every month received the money, giving Nelly back a shilling out of every pound for spending. Mostly it went on presents and the rest was saved.

In weeks, months and years of teaching, as she grew from a girl of seventeen to a small, slim, busy woman in her twenties, Nelly never tired of the school and her children. Years later, when they were old folk themselves, they would always call to see the 'Miss Riley' they remembered. She had a surplus of boys among her scholars: Frank Shepherd now, she could never have hit that lad whatever he did. He had such sheepish eyes. When he opened them wide, and smiled his sweet smile, she knew that he had been particularly wicked. He was most charming on the morning when he had let Bradley's cows out into the village street to enjoy the flowers round people's front doors. Frank brought her a little bunch of wild flowers himself before Mr Longtoft hauled him outside by the ear. Frank was a true romantic, an early admirer in the years before she met Will Mason.

Nelly was learning continually and qualification seemed always far away, but that was to be expected. Twice a week she took the evening train to Skipton, watching Thornton Station flash past her, and got out of Skipton Station by the cattle market to walk along a narrow-boarded snicket and across the canal by the swing bridge to the boys' Grammar School. There she was taught new and difficult subjects never heard of at school: algebra, decimals and geometry.

Laboriously she wrote down the master's instructions word for word in her best hand. In the evenings, after days at school, and with the usual struggle over Professor Elliot's *Geometry and Mensuration*, Dad sat beside her with his mug of tea and showed her how to make the figures. He was always good at setting things out and often understood the real use of some odd mathematical principle. 'Look, Nelly,' he would say, 'here's a wheel. Look at all them spokes. Every one has the same angle where it hits t'bush. It doesn't matter how big you make the wheel, the angles are always the same.' Nelly would brush back her hair and sigh.

She enjoyed the journeys to Keighley Mechanics' Institute every Saturday morning in term time among a little group of assistant teachers. They all talked with grave importance of their course, the examinations, and practical experience, gathering round the carriage window and looking out over the Aire Valley as it passed by. Despite their seriousness they found it impossible not to giggle at each other as they unwound their long grey skirts to present themselves in white blouses, long white knickers and black woollen stockings before the physical education instructress. When it was over Nelly pinned her skirt back on and smiling, flushed, and healthy, gathered her books together for the walk back to Keighley Station. She was happy every day with her flock of children, and she came home in the evenings to the fireside and her books. As Dad and the boys played parchesi and whist in the front room, Nelly stretched out her toes to the fire and sank without trace into Dickens or Harrison Ainsworth.

Time passed. The Boer War had come and gone. Nelly turned out with all the village girls to wave handkerchiefs and cheer when young Eddie Bond and George Nightingale rode off to fight. Two years later the whole village welcomed back a pair of suntanned men to ordinary life. Bonfires blazed on Thornton Moor to celebrate the Relief of Mafeking. Nelly noticed the wrinkles growing on her Mam's face, and the slow, bent way she moved early in the morning until her joints had loosened up. Mam was only fifty. Grandad Riley, in his seventies, still walked his postal round every day. He left the workshop to Bushman, who drank and behaved like a mere lad of thirty. Mam was having to wait a long time for the Post Office.

12

Will

Wright-Jack delivered the first big, cream envelope to Nelly just as she was preparing to leave for school. 'That's a fine-looking outside,' he remarked, 'I wonder what's within.' Nelly clutched the envelope under her arm, determined not to tell, and took it to open on the way. After all, she knew Will Mason's writing. They had been courting for over five years, since she was twenty-one. And last night, before he left, Will had winked as he said mysteriously, 'Now you keep two waltzes for me, won't you, Nelly.'

She sat on her favourite stile and opened it, to find as she had expected a handsome embossed card. It was a three-shilling ticket to the Boxing Day dance at West Marton, marked with spaces for a lady to enter her partners for the various dances. Sure enough, the supper dance and the last waltz were filled already with his name, Will Mason. Nelly sat and thought back for a moment to when they had first met.

She had come to the foot of the embankment steps at Earby Station, when a young man with moustaches and a hook nose, and smartly dressed as railwaymen always were, offered to carry her bag. He followed her along the platform keeping his eye on her face until she turned away and looked down sideways at the iron rails and oil-stained sleepers. Then he said, 'I've seen thee at Earby church in the evenings.' 'Maybe,' she said, for Nelly had promised the curate to attend a few services and sing in his new choir. The railway-man looked seriously down at her with steady blue eyes. 'I'll be there,' he said. 'I'll wait for thee.' Nelly, just a little embarrassed, said as the train whistled and hissed into the station, 'I don't come for every service.' 'Never mind,' was the reply as he helped her into the compartment, 'I'll still be there.' He closed the door and waved to her, one quick friendly signal, before she left.

That Sunday, as she sat on the wooden benches in the choir of Earby's tin chapel, Nelly found herself singing self-consciously. She had watched herself in the mirror at home, and had noticed then the frowns, the outstretched neck and the flushed cheeks as she sang. Now she felt the pair of eyes on her face. If she could have seen the grave but half-excited light in her own eyes, the lustre in her hair from candle-light she would have been more delighted and less anxious. He was sitting in the gallery at the right-hand side and looked down towards her throughout the service. She was forced to keep her eyes on her music. 'He does go on,' she thought, determined not to be a romantic, even if Will Mason was. She had found out his name from Alan, who now worked at Thornton Station.

Will caught her arm as she followed behind the crowd to the door, not lingering, but not pushing to be first either. 'I told thee I'd be here.' 'Well, so you are.' Perhaps that was too sharp, she thought, and softened it with a half smile. 'Aye, and so are you.' He was no fool then. They both relaxed and grinned. Nelly said, 'I must be off home, me Mam's not well. She couldn't come tonight with her bad leg.' Will said, 'I'll see thee home.' She looked sideways at him teasingly, her newly-curled ringlets thrown back over her shoulder. 'Well, if you need a walk.' Will took both the hint and her arm and as they climbed to Thornton he told her about himself.

He came from the remote country below Ingleborough, the wild and bleak fells, source of the River Ribble. His mother died when he was a boy of eight and his sisters, as they grew older, took it in turns to be housekeeper before each married and went away. Will used to trot in his clogs the three miles to school carrying a can of cold tea for all the children. He and his friends went hunting for rabbits in the narrow crevices between slabs of limestone rock, among the thousands of acres of empty land. But when he grew up there was no work for him except on the line. Born and bred beside the great viaduct across Ribble Head, where forty men had died in the building, he joined the Midland Railway and worked his way along it.

Nelly grew to respect Will's serious and solid nature. He was not as light-hearted as her Dad, not as gay when in the mood, but she could trust him. He would always be there and he had his own quiet humour, the jokes and little teasing remarks, as he pulled his nose and his eyes twinkled, which soon brought them close. Nelly, small and trim when she stood beside him, found herself quicker witted, the sharper of the two and able to enjoy herself without care and obligation, relying on Will.

Mam wouldn't let the girls have men friends in the house, not till they had a ring on their finger. That was to be expected in any respectable village household. So, in the five years before they got engaged, Will and Nelly had to invent a life of their own in the world outside Love Tree Cottage. On summer evenings and weekends they took long walks over the hills. In winter Nelly joined a choir and sang in all the neighbouring villages. Her voice was still high, clear and true, and she was generally asked to sing solos, whether hymns or love songs. Folk shouted out for 'Star of Bethlehem' or 'Flow Gently, Sweet Afton' and they listened like William Edmonson with his 'Give us that song to reach me heart'. Will would wait for her outside the house and take her music as they set out for the evening. He stood proudly at the back of the room as she sang, quietly passing *Hymns and Songs for Mission Services* to her, the page ready open for

'Come to the Saviour, Come to the Saviour, Thou sin-struck offspring of man'. Will was not a hasty, nor a demanding man, but he was sure and safe and content with the pleasure of little things.

Nelly sighed happily, then suddenly leapt off the stile. As she hurried along to school, she thought, 'I'll need a new dress.' It was weeks later, only a month before Christmas, when George Elliot arrived on the carrier's cart from Skipton with his box of materials and trimmings. Dark and dapper enough to look middle-aged at thirty, he spread out samples and material. His inexhaustible hamper had buttons, needles, threads, lace and trimmings of all kinds. Sarah had been a valuable customer for years. He always called at Love Tree Cottage and brought what materials the season demanded. Nelly bought five yards of pink voile, and Mam, who worked less now that the children brought in money, made her a tight-waisted, high-necked dress with long sleeves. When Nelly tried it on before the fire her Dad nodded his head with pride. She was a fine lass, a credit to them.

On Boxing Night the dance party set off gaily along the road to Marton. The men carried tin lanterns with candle ends, the girls had dancing slippers in net bags. They hitched up their dresses under their coats and fastened the belts tight to keep them out of the dirt. The sound of their clogs echoed back at them from the row of houses. Everything was ringing cold, white, frosty and beautiful under the rising moon. It was a brisk walk of four miles along the little road to Marton, past the canal thinly coated with shining ice. They were glad to see the glow of lights shining on the frosty road and a warm gust of air met them as they opened the door, and lights, decorations, brightly-coloured dresses flashed in their faces and welcomed them from the darkness and cold outside.

Busily they pulled off coats and scarves, spinning round to spread dresses again and see them flare. The pink voile

141

looked beautiful, not a crease, and Nelly kicked off her clogs quickly to slip on dancing pumps. Candlelight filled the room, a long white table near the door spoke to them of supper to come. Marton folk came over to welcome them. 'Hello, Nelly, where's Will then?' 'Oh, he's still working. He's coming after.' The pianist rose from his chair to announce 'Ladies and Gentlemen. The Chorister's Waltz'. Off they went, violin and piano together, and the dancers went off too, swishing across the floor in long dresses, lace, wing-collars, waistcoats, white gloves and all.

Will arrived just in time for supper, and Nelly ran to meet him, flushed and smiling, her eyes bright. He bent to kiss her and his frosty moustache tickled her ear. She broke away, giggling, took his glowing hand and pulled him inside. They had a bite to eat and a drink of tea, a slice of cake under the candles by the piano. Will pulled on his gloves in preparation for the dancing. The evening vanished almost as fast as the supper. Before they knew it the last waltz was announced and then they were taking off their pumps and putting on their clogs. Now the moon was high in the sky. They clattered merrily down the hill, arm in arm, and turned the corner towards Thornton. It was a shame to go to bed. The whole world was shining silver and every fretted blade of grass and old dry leaf sparkled in the frosty moonlight.

She and Will let the others draw ahead, to wander through that white world alone, pressed close to each other for warmth. Will hummed a waltz tune thoughtfully before he spoke. 'I reckon we've been waiting long enough, love.' Nelly turned her head against his shoulder, 'Shall I ask thy Mam and Dad? I'd like us to get wed soon.' And Nelly, the quick-witted one, could think of nothing to say. She turned her face right against his rough coat and couldn't stop the tears in her eyes. She smiled in agreement and kissed him, 'Let's wait till spring, Will. Mam may be better then.' Ahead, they could hear Annie complaining about the cold and Percy Hartley coughing into his muffler. Mabel Riley shouted back, 'Come on you two.'

Now the church was on their left. Clear stars covered the sky. In the churchyard every gravestone had its coating of frost crystals. They stopped and looked, then, still arm in arm, drawn by the magic, they wandered in and perched on the cold stones, looking out across the valley towards the white limestone hills beyond. Will and Nelly sat close to each other, wrapped against the cold, breathing clouds into the air. Then Nelly began to sing. Her clear voice echoed back from the side of the church, 'While Shepherds watched their Flocks by Night' and, as they all joined in, the carol rang out over a moonlit world.

Snow began to fall next day and stuck at once to the frozen ground. It was a hard winter, with deep drifts mounding high over walls and hedges, so that travellers lost the road and floundered deep in the fields. Wright-Jack returned late from his postal rounds, exhausted, with chapped hands and ears, his trouser legs soaked. He was full of news, as he steamed and coughed by the fire. Edmund Cowgill had been out all night searching for sheep when Wright-Jack met him in the early morning. 'T'were like a scene from the Bible,' he said, 'to see him stagger along with t'sheep over his shoulder.' Nelly had a sudden vision of her Grandad, with his stick and cape, approaching Edmund Cowgill like a minor prophet. But Wright-Jack was over seventy, and the regular exposure began to make him ill. He coughed and coughed, sat close to the fire, and had to be dosed with brandy.

The wet, horrid thaw that followed, when gutters ran with muddy water and soaking rain fell day after day, finally brought a crisis. Wright-Jack developed bronchitis. Bushman walked the postal round. After a family conference between Grandma and Sarah it was decided that the time had come. The old folks would retire, leaving shop and Post Office to their children. Grandma took on the task of obtaining approval from the landlord and a recommendation from the rector.

Nelly returned in the dark one evening to find her Mam staring into the fire. 'Whatever's the matter, Mam?' she said. But Mam just shook her head and put her hands over her eyes. Nelly sat beside her and laid an arm across her Mam's shoulder. Dry sobs began to shake her body as her daughter's comforting relieved the strain. 'Nay, Nelly,' she said, 'I did want you and Will to move in here, right next door.' And so the story came out. No one would recommend Bushman. He was thought too irresponsible to be postmaster. Since Post Office and shop went together they must lose the shop as well. That was the end of Sarah's dreams of security in her old age. Fine house, regular income, even the prospect of a pension, all were gone. She looked forward without hope. When the children were married she would have only Bushman to rely on.

Mam found it more of an effort to face this disaster than Harry Bell's death. But as spring came she began to prepare, gradually taking on more dressmaking, working into the evenings again, and rubbing her tired, dark-rimmed eyes as she laboured downstairs in the mornings. Nelly's announcement of her formal engagement to Will passed almost unnoticed in the general depression. It was not unexpected. Bushman asked, 'Is t'day fixed?' and Will replied, 'We're looking at Procter's house up Cam Lane. If they move in summer we may wed before Christmas.'

Nelly's second big cream envelope was delivered by the new postmaster, a distant cousin from Lancashire. Grandma had managed to keep the post in the family. Nelly carried it carefully down Station Hill to show Will as soon as he left work. When she saw him she let the slope take over, walking faster and faster until her legs broke into a run to keep up. Will stopped solidly, with his feet planted firmly in the gravel, until she ran into him. Then they set off up the hill, Nelly hanging on to his arm. Triumphantly she pulled the letter out of her pocket and took the embossed card from inside it. 'What do you think of this?' Will stopped and looked at it, his back to the sunset. It was addressed to Miss Ellen Cowgill Riley. That was clear enough, but the meat of it, the good news, expressed in stilted copperplate, which Will took time to decipher, was a request that Miss Riley would be present for the formal opening of the New Infants' School, Salterforth. It implied, as they both knew, that she would have a permanent assistant teacher's place, and they could look forward to a busy, useful, married life. Nelly would have her own class room and a crowd of little five, six and seven-year-olds all to herself. What could be a better wedding present? Will said, 'It's just what you wanted, Nelly,' and his smile grew until it vanished in the ends of his moustache. Then Nelly said, 'Let's go and look at the house, Will, just for a minute. I'll make your tea after.'

They walked down the road and turned up Cam Lane under the trees, until at the corner they faced the little house. Mrs Smith had agreed at once to let them have it, now that the Procters were moving. It had been worth waiting for their wedding. After all, they had no reason to hurry. Light fell evenly from a high, blue sky, casting hardly any shadows, but the odd three-storey stone building, backed up against its hillside, seemed to be leaning forward. A long sloping garden followed the road. The house certainly did not look large, but it had two attics, a main bedroom taking up the whole middle floor, a back kitchen, and a living-room in front.

Will and Nelly were delighted with it. They talked over the fifty pounds each they had saved up over the years. They had planned every piece of furniture and looked at wallpapers until the house was rebuilt and decorated in their imaginations. It really only needed their own married shapes, sitting at either side of the fire, to make it complete. There would be oilcloth and tatted rugs in the bedrooms, rush-matting on the flags downstairs, solid brown chairs and settees, and a new iron range in the kitchen to form the centre of their home. Satisfied with the complete and perfect dream they turned and walked back to Love Tree Cottage and a late cup of tea together. Even for such a patient couple the time had begun to drag. Soon they would be married and the dream could become reality.

13

Death and a Promise

One June evening Nelly cleared away the tea dishes as she waited for Will to call after his shift at the station. It was still light and sunny out in the back yard and Dad had gone into the workshop to tidy up a little and shape some timber for next day. Low western sunlight came right through the double doors and warmed the stony depths of the workshop. Half of Dad was brightly lit and edged in gold, the other, shadowy, half was invisible from the yard. His bisected figure worked steadily at the bench and, as he planed, his right elbow moved in and out of the pool of light in an odd fashion, like a mechanical ghost.

Mam came through into the kitchen from the front room. She was limping a little and bent down to touch her sore leg. She had been ill and getting worse lately and her leg made her clumsy and gave her pain. She moved past the table towards the fire and turned to speak to Annie, but as she turned her sore leg caught against the curved rocker of the fireside chair. She closed her mouth again and her face went dead white as she collapsed on the settee in silent agony. Nelly hurried over. 'Has Dr Stone given you nothing for your leg, Mam?' 'Nay it's not so bad, lass. He said to use a poultice, but I think I'll try the sugar again.'

Nelly nodded and went off down to the larder, coming up with the remains of a loaf of sugar and the big rolling-pin. She put the lump on to the scrubbed table-top and tapped it severely several times until wide cracks appeared and large fractured white pieces fell away. Then she pressed her full weight, with both hands on the rolling-pin, and crushed the sugar into powdery crystals. Mam rolled down her stocking and looked at her swollen calf. The long sore ran right down to the ankle, black and hard at its edges and pink and grey where the unhealed flesh filled the inside. A trickle of blood oozed from where the rocker had caught it. Nelly could see it was getting worse rather than better.

She went to the linen bag hanging behind the door, took out the remains of an old sheet, and tore off a long strip for a bandage. Then Mam laid her leg across the chair and, with a spoon, scooped up the sugar and carefully laid it on the wound. She spread it all over with a light hand until the bare flesh was covered. Then she nodded at Nelly. Nelly firmly bound the bandage round the leg and tied it, while Mam lay back and closed her eyes, clasping her hands tightly all the while. She sat still for a moment, her face more grey than white. Then she said weakly, 'I'd better be off to bed,' and pulled herself up slowly and climbed the stairs.

Nelly listened from beside the kitchen table as she heard the footsteps move unevenly into the front bedroom and the creak of the bed as Mam lay down. She was definitely getting worse. Dr Stone had come now and then, but he didn't seem to be able to help at all. Dad would not do anything, whatever was said, except 'Leave it to the doctor,' so it was up to her. What could she do? Medicine was a mystery to everyone, and doctors had their own strange ways of doing things, but she would at least speak to Dr Falconer. He was well thought of in Earby and it would be worth it, even if it did cost money. It was better than sitting worrying while Mam suffered.

Mam refused to be good about her own illness. She hated spending money on doctors and objected to all the fuss. She had expected to keep working like a machine, day in and day out under the pressure of her own determination. Her leg was very sore, but clearly the illness was more than that. Why would the sore not heal? Mam had had bad legs for years now. She never looked really well, and they all knew she had trouble with her bladder. Nothing much could be hidden from such a close family, although they were discreet enough. That was the only way you could live all together in a small house. Nelly observed and thought more than most.

Generally Mam could be relied on for clear common sense, and it was Dad who liked romantic nonsense. But her ideas about medicine were so terribly old-fashioned. She would read the old book that must have belonged to her mother. Its broken back made the title, *Domestic Medicine*, almost impossible to read and the pages were stained brown. The very names in the book had an odd ring to them: 'Anodyne balsams, Astringent boluses, Cataplasms and synapisms, Clysters, Decoctions, Fomentations and Infusions.' Perhaps that was why Mam gave them Sweet Nitre for a cold. How it made you sweat. And Dad took a glass of ground ginger and Epsom-Salts for his rheumatism. He used to complain that all he got from it was wind.

Nelly took the book from its place and opened it. Mam had obviously marked the part that dealt with inflammation of the kidneys: 'There is a sharp pain about the region of the kidneys, with some degree of fever, and a stupor or dull pain in the thigh of the affected side. The urine is at first clear, and afterwards of a reddish colour; but in the worst kind of the disease it generally continues pale, is passed with difficulty, and commonly in small quantities at a time. The patient feels great uneasiness when he endeavours to walk or sit upright.' It did sound very much like Mam. Now what was the treatment? Nelly picked her way through the old-fashioned language, the suggestion that ten or twelve ounces of blood could be taken from an arm or a foot or that leeches be applied to the veins. What was this? 'Emollient clysters ought frequently to be administered; and if these do not open the body, a little salt and honey or manna may be added to them.' This would never do. No wonder Mam was getting worse. She must speak to the doctor the very next day.

She drifted thoughtfully through into the empty front room, where Mam's dresses no longer covered the table. With the children's earnings, and her own illness, Mam could afford and manage to do less, though she still worked whenever she could. Bushman's failure to get the Post Office had forced her to start work again, to take on more commissions and buy in material. It had been too much for her. Nelly resolved to take her Mam in hand.

In the sunshine, next afternoon, Nelly set out to walk back from school. Instead of making for the sloping footpath through Salterforth and her way to Thornton she turned the corner for Spenhead Farm and followed the gravel road to Earby. Once in the town, among lines of terraced houses, she went to the doctors' surgery door, knocked, asked for Dr Falconer, and as he poked his head round the door she quickly began to speak. Would he come and see her mother. No, she was not his patient, she was Dr Stone's. But mother was not getting better and Nelly would like Dr Falconer to have a look. He thought for a minute, then told Miss Riley that he would speak to his partner and would certainly be over in the evening to see Mrs Riley.

Nelly continued along the road beside the railway line, along the last stone terraces of Earby and up the hill towards home. It had been less difficult than she expected and she had heard Dr Falconer arranging for his horse to be readied for the visit. 'How's Mam?' she asked, as she came through the kitchen door. Florrie, the work-house child that Mam had taken in as her own children grew up, ten years old now, was alone in the kitchen, heating some milk in a pan. 'She's in bed, Nelly, she says her back hurts, and she's got pains in her hands and feet.'

Nelly went straight upstairs. The air was hot and close under the low ceiling, with a fire burning in a small grate against the far wall. Mam's eyes were closed, but she opened them when Nelly bent over her. 'Oh lass, back home already? I meant to be back down again before you came.' She began to flounder over the soft mattress with the obvious intention of getting up. Her breath came thickly as she moved, and she winced when her bad leg caught the twisted bedclothes. Nelly gently held her back. 'Nay, Mam, I'll see to dinner. Don't you stir. Is there anything I can get?' 'Well, lass, I do fancy a glass of lemonade. There's a jugful in t'pantry.' Nelly went down to the cool, whitewashed pantry and came back with both a blue jug and a glass to put beside the bed. It was a recognition of permanent illness when meals and drinks had to be taken in bed. The whole process of trays, broths and bedpans had begun.

Dr Falconer arrived as it was getting dark. Dad, in tie and waistcoat, opened the door and welcomed him in, and they went quietly upstairs together. The children could hear muttering voices, the occasional quiet word from Mam and then the heavy sound of boots echoing down the steep stairs and moving slowly through the front room to the door. 'There's very little I can do, Mr Riley. We must just make your wife comfortable where she is. I'll call again tomorrow.'

When Dad came back into the front room he looked quietly round at the children as if asking them to speak. 'How is she, Dad?' Alan got the first word in. Dad sat down mechanically, and put his hands on his knees. 'Doctor says he thinks it's Bright's Disease. Trouble with the kidneys. There's nothing much he can do.' 'Has he left no medicine?' said Nelly. 'Nay, all he said was to keep her in bed and give her plenty to drink.' They all sat in silence for a moment, then Dad came out with the words which seemed to seal Mam's fate in all their minds. 'I think Nelly'll have to give up teaching.'

That night, as she lay in bed, Nelly found it very hard to bring all these thoughts together in a way which eased her mind. Even when she repeated the quiet words of hymns until they echoed through her head she could not get to sleep. To give up teaching, when she had just been given a new post, her own class-room, her own children to watch and teach? And what about Will in his lodgings down at Earby, with the marriage as good as fixed and the cottage up Cam Lane already spoken for? How would she arrange things with him?

Her mind kept going back to the history lesson of that very morning, to the old myth which she had explained to the children, of how in early times men had thought that the world was a flat disc, standing on the back of a giant tortoise. Mam was their family tortoise, who kept them supported, made sure things were provided. How could they fill her place? The house and village were silent. She could hear Annie breathing into the pillow beside her. Dad seemed to have settled down in the boys' bed. The sky outside was only half dark when Nelly closed her eyes.

She felt tired next morning, sitting for a while on the warm stone stiles and turning her face to the sun, before reluctantly marching on. Children who tugged her skirt got a quick tap on the head, and there was no smile for boys who jumped out suddenly at her. After prayers she went up to the front of the class. 'Mr Longtoft, can I have a word, please?' 'Of course, Miss Riley.' Nelly, not fully reconciled to the difficulties, had been going over the necessary phrases in her mind. 'It's my mother. She's getting worse. Doctor says it's Bright's Disease, and my Dad would like me to stop at home to help.' She looked depressed, weary and unhappy, a complete contrast with her usual chirpy self. Mr Longtoft sympathized at once. 'I'm sorry to hear it, Nelly,' he said and took hold of her arm to lead her to the doorway. 'Now you go home at once. You'll be no use here while you're worrying about your mother. We can manage. Come back at the end of the week and let me know how things are going. Don't worry.' Then, jokingly, 'We can't start the new school without you, you know.' Nelly nodded throughout, picked up her hat and coat, and started back along the lane. As soon as she turned the corner she burst into tears.

When she got back Mam looked worse than ever. The final collapse into bed, after she had driven herself to work all these years, was almost complete acceptance that her body's strength was worn out. Nelly sat with Mam in the evenings as she drowsed, turned and muttered. When Mam was delirious, and the family had to sleep, Nelly stayed up late to soothe her. There she sat in the dark room, with only a small lamp beside the bed, the fire dying and Dad asleep among his sons in the big bed against the back wall. Shadows from lamp and fired moved gently till the flames died down, creating odd shapes, constantly catching the corner of her eye to some sudden apparition. The sound of the American clock echoed up the stairs, and she heard an occasional restless stir as Mam turned and breathed shallowly in her bed.

Tonight she dreamed, and spoke, though Nelly could rarely hear what was said. But one old phrase came clearly, or clear enough for Nelly to understand. Mam said it fiercely, as if fighting an enemy, as though somehow Dad had been her opponent all her life. 'If they bury thee on top of me, I'll push thee off.' It came out as a broken sentence, pieced together by Nelly's mind, but Mam kept repeating the words, twisting herself up the bed and getting louder. The boys began to stir, and Nelly took hold of her Mam's face, turned it into the pillow and stroked her forehead until she was at peace again.

Nelly was sitting beside her Mam again later in the week well after dinner and she could hear the mutter of family voices from below. Upstairs everything was quiet. Mam's eyes were open, looking at the ceiling. She turned slowly to Nelly, murmured something and began to lever herself up the bed. Nelly looked up from her book as she caught the change in the laboured breathing. 'Nay, Mam, lie still.' Mam seemed more awake than she had all day. 'Nelly, lass, help me up. There's something I've to say.' 'You're not fit, Mam;

can't it wait?' Mam fixed her bright sunken eyes on Nelly's face and waited for her to rise, lift the pillows, and drag her up the bed. Then Mam feebly patted the pillow for Nelly to sit down on the bed beside her. Mam's breathing slowed down again and she opened her mouth. 'Now, Nelly, I want thee to remember what I say.' 'I will, Mam.' 'Tha must promise me to stay at home and look after t'house when I'm gone.' 'Nay, Mam,' said Nelly; she had been half expecting this but had no easy answer ready. 'I'm afraid of your Dad. He can't look after t'money. He'll be selling things off. He . . .' Her voice died away and she looked towards the side of the bed where Bushman had slept for the last thirty years. Nelly knew that long history of care, of work, the fierce determination to keep house and family together. Now it was being handed on to her. She didn't want it. She had her own future before her. But what could she say? Mam's strong will shone through her sick eyes as she clutched Nelly's hand. What could Nelly say? 'Aye, Mam, I promise.' What else?

Mam's face smiled for a moment. 'There's a good lass,' she said as her hand relaxed. Both sat with their thoughts until Mam turned again to her. 'Tha must look after t'family, Nelly,' and then perhaps in sympathy, 'Will'll understand, he's a good man.' Then Mam closed her eyes. Nelly desperately wanted to go to her own bed and have a quiet, lonely cry; instead she smoothed the sheets, slid her Mam down the bed and sat again on the chair.

This time, when Nelly crept into bed beside her sister, she knew that all her hopes and dreams were to be taken up to the green churchyard with her mother. Her promise was given. There would be no quiet class-room with white walls and busy children; no small cottage of her own and husband to herself beside the fire. She found it so hard to kill the future dreams, to stop her thoughts turning to the house up Cam Lane and planning the furniture, or even picturing her wedding in the old church. Next day, as the afternoon sun filled Mam's sickroom and she looked out at the green love tree, Nelly felt despair. She had no desire to read, no interest in the busy village outside. Why ever had she promised? Her thoughts went round the same laboured circle and, without conscious effort, she moved her head to frame tree patterns in the window.

Still it took time, even to imprison her mother and herself. Mam got steadily worse. She spoke very little, though sometimes her feverish eyes followed people about the room. Every day the sun shone outside and the bedroom became unbearably close. But every day they lit a fire in the grate. Mam wouldn't eat but she drank gallons of lemonade. Dad always got up first to light the fires, and it was one cool morning, as he bent over his wife, his shirt-tail between his legs, that he noticed her absolute stillness. So he crept round to the back room and shook Nelly out of her tired sleep. Nelly came in and stood beside the bed. She touched Mam's face. It felt cold. She touched her shoulder and said 'Mam', but there was no reply. Neither of them could detect any breathing. Nelly straightened her back, sighed and said 'We'd better send for t'rector.'

The ashes were in the fire, the chamber-pot was under the bed; nothing else had changed. The men had to be fed and sent to work. Florrie ran off to school. Only that night, as they went late to bed, could Nelly and Annie have a proper sob together over the death of their mother. Bushman, for all his lightheartedness, was too deeply shocked for tears. Another anchor had vanished from his life. Nelly remained in charge. There was a procedure to deal with the situation and they were certainly prepared. The rector came down and confirmed arrangements for the funeral. Mam's death created no horror, for they had no need to lay out a distorted and agonized body or change it into grave clothes. As always, Mam was prepared, in her good nightdress, relaxed, with her eyes closed.

The family also had prepared themselves for Mam's death

after she began to get worse. Once Nelly took charge they felt that everything could go on as before. Mam was laid out in the front room so they all sat in the kitchen, Dad the most quiet, looking into the fire. He wouldn't make the coffin, so Charlie Watson did it for him. It was just like Dad to train Charlie for nothing and then let him take over all the work. They carried Mam shoulder-high up the village to the dark church, and then earth closed in the neat hole under a mound of soil. Nelly went back to make a funeral tea for all her relatives and family. All of them were there, and all with black, serious clothes and heavy faces. They ate a heavy tea too, and Nelly was busy enough seeing to all their appetites. She had received a letter from Mr Longtoft that morning asking how things were and how soon she would be back. It was a pleasant welcoming letter and, of course, it made her feel even worse. She would have to write and tell him that she must stay at home. Now some of the relatives were leaving, Aunt Mary Ann Rycroft and Uncle Tom, Aunt Sarah and Uncle Stiven. She stood beside Dad on the steps, hot sunshine falling on her black bodice and skirt, emphasizing the white face and steady hazel eyes above. Then she turned to disappear into the gloomy front room.

The house was very quiet in the evening. Nelly sat in front of the fire on the hard chair, thinking of what would happen next. The future had died with her promise to her dying mother. Pleasures and hopes must be given up, however much it hurt; there were new duties to begin at once. The house felt empty, full of dark, demanding, shadows. As the coals in front of her died down her head sank on her hands. She thought for a while. Then she got up slowly to creep to bed, ready for work in the morning. 'Will'll understand,' Mam had said before she died, 'he's a good man.' And Will did understand, even though it meant more solitary days for him in his lodgings down in Earby. The other members of Nelly's family weighed upon her, for if they were close in sympathy they were also close physically in the house.

Reuben and Alan, while in working clothes on their way to the mill, offered to pay twelve shillings a week for their board. Annie thought her eight shillings a week generous.

Mam had said, 'Send our Florrie back when I'm gone,' but Nelly could never bring herself to do it. When Florrie left school and went out to work as a maid she paid her three shillings and sixpence a week and did, in her own dull way, what she could about the house. As soon as Florrie reached seventeen and was able to earn a decent wage, her drunken parents in Skipton claimed her back. She went without a thought, like the sulky pudding she was, leaving Nelly with a houseful of men to provide for. But that was in the future, in the meantime Nelly kept her.

Dad, at fifty-five, with his fine moustache, his weakness for drink and cards, was a problem Nelly did not like to think about. What would he do? Almost every day, knowing of her anxieties, and worried about his own position, he would say: 'It's all right, Nelly, as long as you keep a home for me.' He only tried once to sell off the furniture and Nelly soon put a stop to that. The business had declined since Grandad Riley retired, and all Bushman's expectations had been upset when he was refused the job of postmaster. Bushman was uncertain again, slightly desperate, as he had been after his son Hugh died. He stayed out of the house and worked in the yard. Nelly could see why Mam had been so worried. She had no choice but take her mother's place and worry too.

14

❧

By the Batty Wyf Hole

Bushman rolled his shirt-sleeves up high over the elbow, hung his jacket on the back of a chair and then said, 'Nelly, I'm ready,' as he had done every Thursday since Sarah died. Nelly rattled up from the cellar with the enormous brown crockery bowl, rolling-pin and extra cake tins inside it. She put it down on the table. The sack of flour was already bulging against the table leg. Flour, salt, water and yeast, she scooped them all in and Dad got to work. Soon he was white to the elbows and a fine dust of flour had turned his moustache from grey to white. He blew out a little feathery cloud of it over the table-top. Nelly was laying out the baking tins. They would get through thirty pounds of flour that day and it was going to be hot. The fire in the front room had settled down well and was glowing steadily. As soon as the black oven gave out heat she had put in the night's dinner, potato pie and rice pudding. Once cooked they would be left in the pantry to be re-heated when the family came back. She looked outside and opened the door. It was sunny and warm, the leaves had not yet turned, and beyond the yard stood the yellow stubble of hayfields.

Dad straightened up his back carefully and brushed down his arms, shaking loose flour into the bowl. His housework was done for the day. Now he could set off to join his mates at the hayfield, to work at a moderate rate and crack jokes with Hartley Procter when he came by. Bushman, though still a craftsman, worked only when the fit took him; Mam's death had depressed him, leading to days of moody sitting by the fire. Nelly watched him walk across the yard with his jacket over his shoulder. They had all been very careful with him after Mam died, and it had been worthwhile. Dad had recovered, now he brooded very little and threw on his jaunty air to deal with his cronies. He disappeared up the lane. She picked up the heavy bowl of dough, covered it with a cloth and put it to rise by the range. It wasn't the best day to be tied to the fire, and she looked reproachfully out as the sun rose higher.

While the dough was rising until it nearly came over the bowl rim, she rolled out jam pasties. There had to be one each for the workers to take with them. Twenty pasties to be rolled and laid out, six to a tin. As she opened the oven door hot air came pouring out. It was middling hot but Nelly held a hand carefully an inch away from the iron wall to take its temperature. It felt hot enough for pasties and she slid them in. Now she had time to roll and mix the round sad cakes and the sweet buns. She worked away, laid them on trays, and then stopped for a drink of lemonade. The pasties filled the house with a sweet smell of baking and, when she lifted out the trays, dark jam bubbled from slits in the top and a black crust formed where it had stuck and burned in the heat. Nelly wiped her face with her apron again and stepped outside to the love tree for a breath of cool air. When she came in she put a little more coal on the fire and gave it half an hour to heat up for the bread. Then she worked through the hot afternoon. There were two tins of cob loaves, then eight double loaves, cooked four at a time. At last two currant loaves went in as the oven was cooling and she had the family's baking ready for next week. Now the table-top was covered with knobbly brown bread and pastry, cooling and scenting the air all round. Before she cleared the things away Nelly put the potato pie and rice pudding back into the oven to warm for dinner.

Of course she had no sooner sat down, without spending more than a minute in the sunshine all day, when they all came trooping in. Alan breathed in the air and said, 'Ah, baking day,' and Reuben walked over to finger a good, rounded loaf lovingly. Ten minutes later Annie arrived and, lady-like as ever, went straight upstairs to brush her hair. Nelly and Alan began to lay the table. Then Dad came in, adding the overtones of beer to the bakery smell, and they all sat down to eat – Dad, Nelly, Annie, Reuben, Alan and Florrie, who had come quietly in to help with the table at the end. Nelly looked around at them all, digging into the potato pie; she hadn't much appetite now and was hoping that she might perhaps see Will for half an hour after dinner. She was still sticky from the heat of the fire and could do with a cool evening walk.

There was just one more thing to arrange before she could go out. They would need more soap for wash-day and she asked Florrie to get out the dripping. Florrie came carefully back from the pantry with a tin bowl of dripping and Nelly put it into the oven to melt. As she left the fire and went over to the door she shivered a little. She was tired. Dad had been sent to the workshop for a tin of caustic soda and he stirred a slow stream of crystals into the melted dripping until suddenly it began to turn thick and white. The soap was made. 'Stop,' said Nelly, and Dad stopped pouring. If there was too much soda it took the skin off your hands. Then the bowlful was put aside to set, and the fire left at last to die down into the night.

The weekly routine continued, with washing filling the yard on Monday. It was hot again on Tuesday and yet Nelly had to have a good red fire for the ironing. The coals burned smokily at first and when she stood the flat irons up against the bars of the grate their smooth bottoms became stained with soot and they left black smears on the cleaning cloth. Dad was still shaving in the sink and Nelly asked him to bring some emery paper in from the workshop and scour the irons clean again. He muttered a little through the lather, but it had always been one of his duties. Nelly had started off late and did not seem to be able to catch up. There had been two full lines of washing in the yard the day before, since the men needed two shirts a week for work and sleep. She slipped the felt handle over the first hot iron and held it to her cheek.

She hadn't finished when they came home again, even though her arms were aching and the room was hotter than ever from the fire which had glowed all day. Reuben blundered in and wandered over towards the fireside chair. Nelly was just turning, with a hot, heavy iron fresh from the fire in her hand and there was Reuben, in the way as usual. Obviously he was expecting his tea. 'Get out of my kitchen,' she said sharply just as Mam had done. Reuben looked at her with his foolish brown eyes. 'Nay, Nelly . . .' he bleated, and blundered out again. As a boy he had failed even to drive a nail in to his father's satisfaction and had ended up working in the mill at Earby. He was steady enough to unload the heavy rolls of cloth from the looms. She could hear him lumbering upstairs. Reuben was so clumsy. Still, it was no good letting them get her down. After all, she was much better off than at the mill. Nelly made a resolution to count her blessings.

The family closed in around Nelly and drew nearer to the fireside as winter came. In the long dark evenings they all sat in the front room playing solo whist together and, when the lamp wick burned long and shaky, they called out to Nelly in the kitchen, 'Nelly, there's smuts about.' Since Nelly had the cleaning to do she rushed in to trim the lamp and wipe up the oily smuts before they could stain.

Dad got lumbago and was no help at all. He moaned about his back and said he couldn't carry in the coal when the others were out at work. Dr Stone came to see him and Nelly found she had no patience for either of them. They were both playing games. 'Are you still there, you old devil?' the doctor would say. 'Aye, and I'll be here a bit longer yet,' her Dad would reply. 'Pull up your shirt then,' and this would be followed by a whole series of groans. Then Dr Stone would make his parting remark, 'Well there's only one remedy; rub it well with whisky.' As he stood on the doorstep Bushman shouted after the retreating doctor, 'I'd sooner sup it.'

Tied fast to the fireside, Nelly found it hard to believe that the world outside still existed, that Mr Longtoft skipped briskly about his spanking new school in Salterforth and that children still walked along the lanes, over the hills to school, without Miss Riley's hands to hold and skirt to cling to. But that long winter began to disappear. At least, as mistress of the house, she could have Will in for Christmas dinner, and he made the day brighter. They talked quietly on the settee by the front-room fire and joined loudly in carols as Annie sat at the piano. Nelly regretted having to see Will off into the biting wind, and take a candle up to bed with Annie yet again. She found even less pleasure in making all their breakfasts next morning. But she and Will had been waiting seven years. What was a little more time to them?

When Will was working the morning shift at Thornton Station he came up the hill every afternoon to take tea with Nelly. She would sit, if she could, in the sheltered corner by the front door, waiting in the sunshine for his face to appear up Station Hill. He would cross the road, put his arm round her just inside the front door, give her a kiss and then lay down his bait-box on the dresser as she took the kettle from the fire.

'I've had a letter from me Dad,' he said one day. 'Do you know what he says?' 'No?' 'You'll be surprised.' 'Aye, may be, but why not tell me?' 'He says, why don't we go up to Ribble Head, you and me, to see him. Our Anne'll look after us well enough.' 'Well, I don't know,' said Nelly, as she sat down to take it in. This was an idea that could never even have been mentioned while Mother was alive. Will put his hand on hers. 'It'd do you good to get away.' Then more quietly, and after a short silence, 'It'd do me good too.' Nelly thought of Will's patience, his cheerful acceptance of delays and the destruction of their hopes. She looked up and said 'Aye, Will, let's go.'

It was a cloudy Saturday morning in early April when they walked down the road to Thornton Station, Will carrying both their bags. Nelly found it a real adventure to be setting off to spend a few days away from home. The train was already hissing beside the platform as they arrived, and the station-master came out of his office. 'Morning, Will,' he said, 'I hear you're going up to see old Thomas.' Everyone on the line knew that Thomas Mason had been head plate-layer in the great Blea Moor tunnel when the Midland Railway was carried through the hills to Scotland. He was one of the quiet heroes of those pioneering days. So the station-master added, 'Remember me to your father, Will,' as he saw them off. Will helped Nelly inside and they sat in the carriage facing each other, waiting for the familiar land-scape to draw away.

The line curved along the valleys, skirting the edge of the hills, passing through Long Preston and Settle. Now Nelly could see close in front of her the flat, high, craggy-edged top of Ingleborough, the most distant point to the north if she looked to the hills from Wilson's Fold at home. The train came into a steep-sided valley, Ingleborough to the left with rugged slopes and terraces falling down to the shallow beginnings of the River Ribble, and on the right the high hill of Pen-y-Ghent, a great, steep slope rising towards its top over Mean Moss and Gavell Rigg. Following the river line, by lonely farms and flocks of sheep, the train at last rolled to a stop at Horton-in-Ribblesdale Station where the engine took on water before beginning the lonely run to Carlisle.

Will and Nelly got out and Will popped into the station-master's office to find out what trains were expected down the line the next hour. Then he took Nelly straight out along the railway line. In front of them rose the long grey side of the fells, Winterscales topped by Greensett Craggs, and above them the ponderous slope of Whernside. The railway embankment gradually rose against the grey of the hills. Then they came almost to the edge of a cliff. A great viaduct stretched away above the marshes and their path led along its top. They took the up-line, to leave room for the trains which were coming down into England. Bravely Nelly followed Will along the side of the line, looking over the low parapet wall to the drop below. A strong, bitter wind was channelled up the valley and blew against their faces as they walked.

They had been walking for an hour when Will drew over to the parapet wall. 'There's a train due,' he said. A sea of clouds blew over the summit of Ingleborough and Park Fell, lifting a little as it left the hill-top, and the sky behind shone silver-white. He pointed down the valley. 'There's Batty Wyf Beck, it runs into t'Ribble a bit further down.' Nelly tried to see, but the wind filled her eyes with tears. She peered cautiously over at the rough stones of the viaduct and the great, broad buttresses supporting it. Will blew his nose again. The rails began to sing. 'Must be out of t' tunnel,' he said. A cloud of steam rose in front of them and then the engine appeared round the corner. A great thundering and steaming machine rushed towards Nelly as she crouched back against the parapet wall and quite forgot the drop below. She clutched Will's arm, for it seemed there could hardly be room to escape the onslaught in that narrow way. But the engine passed them, and she caught glimpses of passengers' white faces looking out at them in amazement from the red carriages. Then the train was gone and they could walk again in silence.

As the long stone length of the viaduct disappeared behind them Nelly felt a little safer. The line curved round to the right, into a small valley, and Will pointed out Winter-scales Beck running beside the track and the cutting into Blue-Clay Ridge. He had heard a fund of stories from his father about the great days of railway building. That clay was so hard the navvies had had to blast it out with gunpowder and yet, when it rained, the stuff became like glue and a blow with a pick might loosen a teaspoonful. Men who had built railways all over the country, and even all over the world, left the job in droves. But the line was finished and now they could see the great tunnel leading under Blea Moor.

Just below the tunnel entrance, on a little patch of level ground with the beck nearby, stood a pair of strange black buildings. Nelly looked more closely. They were houses, made of wood and tarred all over. Stranded here on the edge of the great hills as the tide of railway builders had left them, they appeared to be temporary lodgings. But Will said 'Here we are,' and led her down from the line towards a stone stile and muddy path to the black houses. The buildings grew bigger as they approached, being only tiny in proportion to the landscape. They were black and shining as she had first seen them, tarred roof above, tarred slatted board below, but with curtains at the windows, and a few early crocus out around the door. Thomas Mason, his nose even bigger than Will's, opened the door to them and welcomed them in.

After the armies of navvies had left, Thomas Mason had stayed close beside the tunnel which had dominated their lives for so long. It kept him busy enough, for rails corroded after ten years in that smoky, sulphur-laden air. Something grand, demanding and important about the place and the work had kept him there. After hours spent deep inside the hot and airless hill, he would come home to the tunnel entrance and see the green loneliness of open hills and sky, as much air and space as a man could desire. That was why Will, his three brothers and four sisters, had been brought up out here, miles from anywhere with only the hills around them. The house was as comfortable as could have been desired; three bedrooms, a good kitchen at the back, with plenty of hot food, and a fire always ablaze in the front room. 'We've put thee in with Anne,' Nelly was told.

As they sat by the fire and the cold wind blew outside, Thomas Mason told them the tale of the building of that last railway line from Settle to Carlisle, high over the Pennines, in the mountain centre of the North of England. Its building had taken much of the ten years before Nelly was born, as great gangs of navvies worked with their picks and shovels. There were many amazing stories of these men, who sometimes shifted sixteen tons of dry gravel a day and earned ten shillings for doing it. Mr Mason suggested they should have a good look at the viaduct from the hillside, for many men had died in building it; their graves could be seen in the churchyard at Chapel-le-Dale. They built it over bog, rock and clay. It was heart-breaking work in the heavy rains when picks and shovels disappeared in the mud, and the rock that was tipped to form embankments just sank out of sight. Why, they even had bog-carts – drawn by three horses working up to their stomachs – which ran, when they ran, on great round barrels instead of normal wheels. Even so they would stick, the horses would flounder, and men must get into the bog to haul and push them out, up above their waists, losing their boots and sometimes even their trousers.

Thomas Mason drew on his pipe, looked at the warm fire and smiled. 'The way we lived in them days, in t'railway camps.' He glanced around in comfort as the fire shone across to Will and Nelly on the settee, flickered on wall-paper, and lost itself in the dark rugs on the floor.

The biggest camp of all, he told them, had been down there beside the beck. It held two thousand folk, and they called it Batty Green after the Batty Wyf Beck. Those had been rough times. The tarred huts stood on bare earth, with nothing inside them but crude wooden bunks and benches. Old women took charge of the huts, keeping the beer kegs locked up tight with the keys hung on chains around their waists. They stoked the roaring coal fires and saw to the boil-

166

ing cauldrons, for each man's dinner bubbled away in its own string bag or piece of cloth while waiting for its owner to come in. Some of them worked in the seven deep shafts which were sunk from the moor top to speed the tunnel cutting. After a day spent with their picks hewing rock by candlelight they would emerge into a dark, windswept world, to be guided back to camp and their dinner through knee-deep bog by the light of a bull's-eye lantern. There they found, not only beer and hot dinner, but shops, pubs, a school and Post Office. There were muddy paths between the huts and every navvy seemed to have a dog or dogs, mongrels and lurchers. Batty Green was a frontier town.

Great convoys of food, he went on, came up along the line and by road from Settle, for the men ate to match their work. Whole sides of beef were hung up in the tommy truck with its tarred roof, and enormous loaves of bread were baked for them; beer they consumed by the gallon. 'It were a rough life,' he said again, shaking his head. Almost every Sunday men fought bloodily with their bare fists to see who would be Cock of the Camp. They had their own missionaries coming round on horseback from one romantically named camp to another, Sevastopol, Salt Lake City and finally Batty Green.

Old Thomas leant forward, his nose jutting into the firelight, hands on his knees. 'Well, Nelly, dost tha want to hear about one of them navigators? They called t'work folk navigators in those days.' 'Is it true?' said Nelly with interest. Thomas nodded slowly but Anne corrected her father, 'He's been telling those tales for thirty years or more and they've grown bits here and there. It's not right truth, not all the way through.' Thomas glowered at her, but spoke to Nelly. 'Dost'a want to hear? Right.'

'He were called Wellington Pincher. A big bony face he had, with great big mucky cauliflower ears and hair in them. He only shaved his face, and not under his chin, and his thick beard stuck over his shirt collar – when he wore a collar. He used to cut the ragged ends with his clasp knife, or bite them off. You'd see him walking along, his pick over one shoulder, twisting his head sideways to get a good chew on the end of his beard. My, he were a worker though. At shifting gravel he was one of the men who could move sixteen tons a day. He had only one friend, and they shared two bunks, the little fellow on the top one. It were at the end of Dorset Peggy's hut.

'Nay, I don't know anything about the friend, not even his name; it were before my time.' Thomas answered their unspoken questions. 'Anyroad, things were going badly. We had over two thousand men on contract Number One, that's what Midland Railway called it. Nearly all of them lived in the camp by Batty Wyf Hole. We had four locomotives taking wagons to and fro from the tunnel and three mobile cranes. But it rained and rained, ninety inches that year, so they say. Men were blown off the viaduct, and some days it were too bad to start work. We had over a death a week right through the winter. Widows and orphans in the camp, and missionary Tiplady raising collections for them every Sunday. The contractors put up a hospital with a wooden veranda and bought an ambulance, a big canvas-covered wagon.

'Now Wellington Pincher and his mate worked in a gang at the bottom of shaft No. 4, half-way over the moor. They went down in an iron skep, like miners, and worked by candlelight. Generally it were hot, about eighty degrees, and that close and damp you began to sweat and breathe heavy as soon as you reached the bottom. When we cut through at last the temperature dropped twenty degrees in five minutes, but that were later.

'One day their gang were sent on an emergency to Blue Clay Ridge, down the track yonder.' Will and Nelly nodded in understanding. 'A land-slip threatened after all the rain, a great mass of wet clay was about to fall. It still rained as they worked, and they all wore tarpaulin capes. Most of them bought knee breeches and long thick woollen stockings. Farmers' wives in Dentdale used to knit them by the hundred and bring them in to camp to sell. But there was no way of keeping out the rain and mud in that weather and they were all plastered with blue clay.

'They stationed the wagons a bit up line from the clay and most of the gang were sent up top to hack it down in great balls, keeping a watch against the cracks where they stood. They almost had it clear, and the trucks were moved further down to get the last few tons when suddenly a slip started. It were only a small one. They shouted a warning from above and it caught just a couple of trucks and three men. Two of them got out alive, but Wellington Pincher's mate were right below. When they dug out his body his mouth were packed full of clay.

'Wellington Pincher went very quiet for a few weeks. Dangerously quiet he was, then wild. He drank whisky instead of beer and roared around the camp looking for fights, and finding them. It still rained. Men were shut up too long in the huts. They played cards and drank. There were not much else to do. Dorset Peggy put on a navigator's ball with pails full of ale and bottles of whisky. Some men brought their wives. Mrs Pollen even had two grown-up daughters with her. The navvies were generally very respectful to decent women, and there weren't that many of the others.

'Wellington Pincher came in roaring drunk. He picked up a pail of ale and spilt half down himself. Then he tried to get one of Mrs Pollen's daughters to dance, pulling her arm when she clung to her mother. She screamed for help, and Wellington Pincher were knocked down at once and sat on. They threw him out, face down into t'mud. All were quiet and the fiddler started again. Then he were back hammering on the door and charging against it like a bull; so half a dozen of them went out and took him on. They beat his head against the wall till he stopped roaring. Then they poured buckets of water on his head until he broke loose and wandered away. They let him go, went back and danced till morning.

'But Wellington Pincher were never seen again. No one found his body. He was last seen wandering off towards the far end of the camp. Beyond that part were some blind shafts they had sunk early on. They'd been used for tipping clay, and rain had half filled them with water. It's my belief poor Wellington Pincher staggered into the dark night with his head spinning, fell into a blind shaft and drowned. If they tipped next day no one would ever see his body. It would be buried in the clay. He may still lie out there.' Thomas looked significantly towards the window. Nelly shivered at the thought.

The next morning Will and Nelly walked over the crisp grass beside Force Gill. The hills that she had seen in the distance from the crumpled valley at home opened in front of her, high and clear, with here and there a few dots of sheep. Long straight lines of dry-stone walls crossed them, built by gangs of men who slept in the open, found their own material and were paid at sixpence the yard. The beck tumbled down in companionable noise over its little waterfalls. Everything was grey, the sky above and the fellside rising in front of them, except when they turned and looked down to the bright limestone green of the valley grass and the moss beside the becks. There was a biting wind, but that didn't matter in the least.

Will held her hand as they followed broken sheep paths along the water edge. Then pulled her, scrambling, up a rocky slope to pause beside an old bare hawthorn, half blown out of existence by the wind. They stood to catch their breath and look back on the way they had come. Now they could see where Dale Beck ran above the tunnel mouth, carried on its little stone aqueduct. They turned to face the hillside and plodded on towards the slope of Greensett crags and the shallow tarn beyond. When they stopped, half-way up the scree slope, in unspoken agreement, they sat down in a little hollow, edged by dry tussocks of grass, and looked out over the Ribble Valley below. They sat in silence, the wind in their faces, until Will said, 'If we don't wed now, we never will.'

15

Wed at Last

On Sunday Nelly brushed the last tangles from her hair and shuddered as she looked out of her bedroom window in Love Tree Cottage. The warm firelight made that cold grey morning mist look even more threatening, as it clung in droplets to the fat buds of the love tree and shone on the smooth stones round its base. They must go out within five minutes. Church service would never wait. She saw a grey figure appear at the top of Thornton Hill and turn down the slope towards them. Surely it was Will, his railwayman's cape pulled round him? Bless him, he must have decided to come early and meet her at home rather than at church. He wouldn't be able to do that on Tuesday when they got wed at last. The dreadful weather must improve by then, she thought fiercely. Shouting at the family, especially Bushman, who was still lacing up his boots, she got them to the door and opened it to Will. He kissed her cheek, she could feel the damp ends of his moustache. 'Hello, love. I thought we'd go together this time.' They set off, arm in arm, leaving the family to follow.

Everyone moved a little faster at the top of the hill, as the wind began to bite and the mist began to feel more like rain. That four-hundred-year-old grey church, long and rough, partly dug into the ground, seemed to offer little comfort. Waves of mist were blowing over the heavy slabs of the roof and falling as rain on the folk who came to the door.

No one gathered round to talk as they would have done in summer; they pushed in, stamping and blowing and shaking their coats and capes. The Rileys crowded close behind their neighbours, hurrying down the steep, slippery, flag path to the church door. The walls of the church were green and damp in places. Archaic worn faces below the window mouldings dripped grimly on to the grass below. Rain marked the lop-sided carving, the crude tracery scratched out by a remote hill people. In a rough land, living hard, they had laboured together, heaving blocks of local stone into place, building their church close to the ground. It was as solid and rough as themselves.

But the wilder it was outside, the more warm and sheltered folk felt inside. Nelly could see down the grey, dark, close-smelling nave, with ragged-stone pillars running on at either side, and here and there the small rings of candlelight. They passed the servants' pews by the door, and she remembered her unhappy days of work at Fence End House, now long past. Mrs Smith had been dead over five years, nearly as long as the old Queen. At the back, under the tower, where a great uneven arch rose in crude roll-mouldings to support the end of the nave, Mrs Smith had sat, facing down the central aisle to the altar. No earthly inhabitant of the village came between Mrs Smith and her God. The Rileys' family pew stood just behind and Nelly thought of all those childhood Sundays in church. Grandfather and Grandmother, Aunt Lizzie, and the grandchildren, who used to squeeze securely between that mass of black propriety at one end and Mam and Dad at the other, equally black and solemn. Nelly had always huddled close to her mother in the dark, or held Reuben's hand when she was older. All of them had a place in the family pew. The children were grave and quiet. There could be no scuffling of feet or whispering. They were hemmed in by a solemn world.

Nelly knew no other way of arranging the world than this social pattern, frozen like a fragile ice crystal for a few hours

every Sunday, but concealed under the busy surface movement of weekday life. She settled down next to Will, still
half dreaming of the past. From a thick column in the nave a
strange primitive face, carved solid from an octagonal block,
stared at her. When she was a child she had always been
afraid of that face, had turned her head away from it and
buried into Mam's soft arm, only to turn back again, fasci-
nated but frightened. How it moved in flickering candlelight. Its whole aspect, its expressions of love and hate,
contempt, happiness or serenity, changing with every draught
of air. Now it was an old friend, and through its crude, stern,
mask it seemed to smile at her.

Everything was quiet and the wind could be heard rising
outside. Candles glowed brighter and warmer as the nave
grew dark and the light fell. Then the rector's strong voice
rose clearly: 'Almighty and most merciful Father; We have
erred, and strayed from thy ways like lost sheep . . .' Nelly's
lips followed the familiar sentences, leaving her thoughts
behind. Time and again such words of power had been sent
running through her mind until they were fixed deep inside
her. Mr Morris appeared above the shadowy line of pews,
his white surplice blazing in the light of four candles. She
still found it hard to believe that a pair of stout but
invisible legs fixed the ethereal top-half of the rector firmly
to his deal platform. But Mr Morris was getting old, his
voice not always constant, his hunting jacket and billycock
hat put away. Though his face was still red, his hair had
turned white.

Nelly, sitting at the back, could see the whole village in
front of her. The farmers sat in their family pews, even old
Hartley Procter, who still came to play cards with her Dad.
A right pair of old gamecocks, the two of them. She could see
Hartley Procter's shirt collar sticking up even in that dim
light, as if it showed his resentment at having to wear a tie.
Billy-a-Doad, his head nodding just above the pew back, sat
beside the aisle, his married sons and their families filling

two pews entirely. William Edmonson and his wife, a weatherbeaten, upright pair, sat at the front.

The quarrymen were scattered down the sides, bunched close to heating grilles in the floor. There were lads she had been at school with sitting among their children. Frank Brown, still quarry engineer, sat alone, his little, dirty, old mother long dead, and his rough brother, John James, was also dead, killed by a stroke one hot day in the quarry. Nelly thought of John James and his stubborn system of organ blowing. 'John James . . . James, you're going too fast,' would come a desperate whisper from the organist, and in the deep silence, as everyone took breath for the next line, John James' reply echoed round the church, 'I'm blowing for "God save the Queen", tha can play what tha likes.' Now Reuben pumped the organ. He was more biddable.

The rector announced a hymn, and Nelly's mind came back from the past. Soon she was dreaming of the future, of the wedding on Tuesday, and life with Will. They would have to stay at home of course, her promise to Mam still held, and she must look after the family. Love Tree Cottage would be crowded, but at least Dad had agreed they should have the back bedroom to themselves. Mr Morris recited the blessing, and as his voice died away they knelt in silence, listening to the gusts of rain and the wind howling through dark bell slits in the tower. Choirboys snuffed out the candles, filling the nave with shadow, and everyone gathered round the doorway, hesitating on the edge of discomfort. Lines of falling water drove past the beech trees to bounce at regular angles from the flat grey tops of tombs or stream down the sides of gravestones. Families threw capes over their heads, gathered babies close to their skirts, stepped out of the porch, and slithered up the path in tightly packed groups.

The wet Sunday passed, to be followed by a wet Monday. Nelly had gone to bed on Monday night determined to sleep.

She tossed and turned and finally managed to drowse off, but awoke at the first clear light. Now she was happy to lie still in bed as Annie mumbled beside her. Outside she could hear all the first sounds of the village. Calls of the rooks in their high nests soared over the house roof and bounced back at her until the yard seemed full of distant and invisible birds. The first cart rumbled slowly up the road, creaking like a wooden ship, the horse's hooves clanging on the hard surface. Billy-a-Doad's cows bellowed loudly from the shippon. Billy was old enough to take life more easily. His sons ran the farm for him.

Downstairs, Dad was lighting the fire. Nelly could hear the rattle of coal in the bucket and, if she strained her ears, almost catch the sound of him blowing fiercely through his moustache to keep the coal dust away from his face. He must be doing that now, even though he always breathed in the dust harder before he could blow out. Nelly opened her eyes and through a crack in the brown curtains could glimpse the green of the hillside, patches of earth in the garden and bright sunlight on the bare apple tree. It was going to be a beautiful day. Quickly she sat up and looked to the light-brown costume hanging on the wall. Aunt Lizzie had made it for her and it was a professional job, elegant and sensible, better than a frilly white dress which had only one day's life in it and would then be closeted away. It could be worn as best for years after.

Nelly has forgotten everything that happened that morning until they came out of church. She was too excited to notice details and, since nothing went wrong, there was nothing to remember. She found herself hanging on tightly to Will's arm, standing in the sharp sunlight outside the church door, as a flock of birds fought excitedly for grains of rice among the tombstones. They walked to the church gate. The family were behind them, friends and neighbours along the path, and a little knot of children in front. She whispered, 'Have you got some coppers in your pocket, Will?' 'What do I want with coppers, Nelly?' he said. But of course, the gate was held fast closed by the grinning group of children. Will stopped and looked at them, nodding his head in understanding. He put his hand in his pocket and they all stopped chattering, but their grins grew even wider in anticipation. Then Will threw the coins high over their heads into the long grass. The gate was open, children vanished to scramble excitedly in the muddy tussocks. The way was clear.

The wedding breakfast soon vanished. A crowd of guests took them down Station Hill to catch the four o'clock train and waved noisy 'good-byes' with white handkerchiefs as they drew out of the station. Will and Nelly sank into their seats and sighed with exhaustion. The train began to gather speed and whistled down the Ribble Valley, through cotton towns, into the world of red brick, past rows of terrace houses with back yards and coal sheds, alongside mills, mines and chimneys by the dozen. Nelly hardly spoke and Will closed his eyes, but whenever the train stopped at a station they smiled at each other. At length it let them down on the flat coastland by a vast shallow bay in Morecambe.

They would have four whole days on their own; Pancake Tuesday was almost over, but Ash Wednesday, Fritters Thursday, Fish Friday and Anything-you-like Saturday, remained. They walked to the boarding-house. Annie had booked it for them. They lived retiringly and never confessed to be newly married. Will would take a walk in the mornings while Nelly sat knitting. In the afternoons they walked along the promenade and looked at the sea. It was just like being a regular married couple. They had fine cold weather to blow colour into their cheeks, and the four days passed almost instantly. On Sunday morning, as they were about to leave, it began to rain. The landlady saw them to the door and wished Mr and Mrs Mason a good trip back home. On the doorstep Nelly unfastened her umbrella and pushed it up. Out fell a cascade of confetti over Nelly, Will and the landlady. 'Why,' said the landlady, 'Mrs Mason, you've coloured up.' 'I'll colour me brother up too when I get home,' said Nelly.

Their train worked its way back inland towards the hills and home, and at last it whistled into Thornton Station. There were no friends to meet them. They emerged privately as man and wife. Will put the bags on the platform, Nelly picked up her umbrella and looked at it threateningly. The station-master came out of his office, though, and said as they began to climb down from the platform. 'I'll see you on Monday, Will.'

The top of the love tree soon appeared above Station Hill and as they climbed its black irregular framework of branches could be seen, softened by a mist of green buds. They came to the main road and saw Love Tree Cottage again. Will said 'Shall we go round t'back?' 'No,' Nelly replied. 'We'll go in by t'front door.' She marched in with a confident face.

Sunday dinner was over and all the family were by the front room fire, Dad, Annie, Reuben, Alan and Florrie. Alan perked up at once saying, 'They're back!' 'Hello, Nelly, where's Will?' 'Just coming,' Will shouted from behind the front door. Nelly turned towards Alan and waved her umbrella at him, like a schoolmistress with a ruler. 'I've a bone to pick with thee, Alan.' When Alan chuckled in reply it was all Nelly could do to keep a straight face and she marched on up the stairs as Will followed with the bags. The same bedroom, the same brass bed, though Annie's things had gone, but Dad had actually put skirting-boards around the walls against their coming back. And next door a new partition split the old bedroom, where Mam had died, into two. Dad and the boys would sleep just inside the door. Annie and Florrie had their own private room beyond. Now they had three bedrooms for seven folk.

Will and Nelly stood together on the landing, looked at each other and hesitated, until Nelly said, 'Come on, Will.' It was the easiest thing in the world, once she'd put the kettle on and made tea for them all. Soon the kitchen filled with the noise of hot liquid being strained through heavy moustaches. Alan brought in a bucket of coal and stoked the fire. A dank evening mist closed about the house. Bushman raised his grey head from the *Craven Herald*, unbuttoned his waistcoat, and rocked to and fro for a moment before speaking. 'Well, lass, tell us thy tale.'

A CHILD IN THE FOREST

Winifred Foley

'A winner . . . a vivid and personal story of the life and hardships faced by a Forest of Dean miner's family in the 1920's . . . a moving commentary on the Forest way of life as seen through the eyes of a child'
Gloucestershire Life

'A land of oak and fern, of secret hill farms and plain, matter of fact market towns . . . Still a Forester, Winifred Foley recalls vividly but unsentimentally the loving, poverty-stricken home where she was brought up'
Birmingham Post

'Warm-hearted and well-observed' *Sunday Telegraph*

'The story is funny and touching by turns' *Manchester Evening News*

A CHILD IN THE FOREST is the book on which the Radio 4 Woman's Hour serial of the same name and the BBC 1 television film, ABIDE WITH ME, was based.

MILLSTONE GRIT

Glyn Hughes

'The best book I have read on the North of England for some time' *Alan Sillitoe*

'A fascinating insight into the grimmest piece of the Pennines, the open moors, the changing villages and the decayed and decaying scattered dwellings; the raw winters above the towns, the whirling mists lit by shafts of sun, and the beauties seen in the very bleakness' *Oxford Times*

'A grand book . . . the work of a subtle poet with an ear of a standup comic and the eye of the most delicate of water colourists' *The Times*

'Really does capture the substance and spirit of Blake's satanic mills . . . an affectionate evocation of a dour land and an endearing people' *Daily Telegraph*

84 CHARING CROSS ROAD

Helene Hanff

'This book is the very simple story of the love affair between Miss Helene Hanff of New York and Messrs Marks and Co, sellers of rare and secondhand books, at 84 Charing Cross Road, London. It is unmitigated delight from cover to cover.' *Daily Telegraph*

'Immensely appealing . . . witty, caustic' *Listener*

'20 years of faithful and uproarious correspondence with a book-shop in Charing Cross Road' *Evening Standard*

'A lovely read, a must for all who worship books' *Books and Bookmen*

'A delightful story . . . one of the most charming books I have read' *Anne Edwards, Sunday Express*

UNQUIET SOUL

Margot Peters

'A totally fascinating book about the Brontës – perhaps the best ever published' *Irving Stone*

'The story itself is so gripping and the telling is so good that one ceases to question and reads on to weep . . . a most readable book that cannot fail to move' *Margaret Drabble*

'This fine biography is both moving and revealing . . . a compelling narrative, never marred with indiscriminate sympathising' *Spectator*